SONIA LIEBHART AND

DEVIANT ~~dream~~

DOG

**DISCOVER THE DOG OF YOUR DREAMS INSIDE
THE ONE YOU ALREADY HAVE**

ISBN: 978-1-913521-00-4 (paperback)
ISBN: 978-1-913521-01-1 (hardback)
ISBN: 978-1-913521-02-8 (ebook)

Printed in the United States of America.

Cover Design by 100Covers.com
Interior Design by FormattedBooks.com

DEDICATION

To our more challenging canines and their dedicated owners.

ACKNOWLEDGEMENTS

With love and thanks to our family and friends, especially Roxanne Odd, Philip Gray and Kevin Gager-Tomkinson. With a special mention to Stacey Jane Anderson for her generosity in providing the hand-drawn illustrations supporting our work. As well as a big thanks to the team at Absolute Dogs.

QUOTES

Wherever possible, the accuracy of quotes used,and their attribution has been checked. However, in some instances it has not been possible to verify the quote. If the makers of any quotes that have been misattributed or inaccurately presented would kindly notify the authorsof their having been the original author, then they will take all reasonable steps to give the correct attribution on any reprinting.

CONTENTS

PART 4: THE HUMAN END OF THE LEASH

INTRODUCTION

Deviant dog to Dream dog. What does that mean to you?

Imagine your dream dog. Maybe this is your idea of a normal dog? One that is wonderful at home, easy to walk on the lead, greets people and other dogs calmly and will come back when you call.

The 'deviant' dog label perhaps conjures up images of all things you consider 'naughty or not normal'. In this book we will examine such thoughts. If your much-loved dog, Fido, is a hooligan at home, never stops, chews your possessions and has cost you a fortune. If, on a walk, he pulls like a train, is embarrassingly noisy or jumping and spinning when another dog is seen even in the distance. If any of those 'not normal', 'naughty', or; deviant' behaviours apply to your Fido, this book is for you.

Perhaps the 'deviant' behaviour is so extreme, if you believe the stress caused by Fido in your household has reached critical level and seems to be getting worse.

Have you ever considered the painful thought of needing to re-home your precious Fido? Maybe you feel you do not have the time or skills to provide the right home for him. An agonising decision to make because he is a much-loved part of your family.

Do you sometimes feel that your dog is responsible for so much of the stress and arguments in your home because he will not listen, is too excited, never stops barking or has caused so much damage that you are worried to leave him on his own?

Maybe you have no time to socialise with friends as Fido takes up so much of your time and energy. Perhaps you have stopped inviting friends and family because Fido is so difficult. Has your life become restricted? Is going on holiday difficult, or even impossible, to consider?

Are going for daily walks a nightmare of embarrassment and a feeling of failure and frustration? Could it be that your much-loved Fido pulls so much, and you worry that you cannot hold him? Is he too strong for you? Does he choose to bark hysterically, chase children, bikes, skateboards and will not come back? Do you dread the walks and argue about who is going to walk him?

This is not what you envisaged when you signed up for having a dog. In this book, we are going to show you how to creatively turn your struggles into strengths. You can transition from a Deviant to a Dream Dog.

Discover the dog of your dreams inside the one you already have.

The Four Principles for Transformation

1. The dog end of the leash.
2. Managing the environment.
3. Powerful partnership.
4. The human end of the leash.

This comprehensive, integrative approach will address the root of the issue in a compassionate, fun-filled, positive and reward rich way. This will ensure that the awesome results remain and are real life ready, not just in a training class or environment.

We will give you the knowledge and tools to power-boost your relationship. Once you are aware of the four key principles and implement the strategies you will be amazed at how quickly your life together will improve. Techniques are fun, simple and only take a few minutes. You can be the best partner for your dog and provide the best forever home.

Think about why you chose to have a dog. Maybe for companionship, love or enjoyable walks. This can be your reality. Not just a dream.

Our Credentials:

Drawing on forty years of practical experience working professionally with horses and dogs, Sonia has academic (B.SC. Honours: Psychology and Physiology together with a teaching degree) and vocational achievements with numerous Diplomas and foundation degree qualifications in holistic therapies (both human and animal). She also holds qualifications in Neuro linguistic programming, Cognitive Behavioural Therapy and Mindfulness. Vocational qualifications include British Horse Society and other nationally recognised accredited courses. She is a professional dog trainer and has helped hundreds of equine, canine and human partnerships to have their perfect life together; having become Pro Dog Certified in 2018. This together with a passion to help, her lifelong learning and a growth mindset she believes she is in a position to help.

Like everybody, she has made mistakes, followed the prevailing wisdom of the time, and now knows better so can do better. She aims to integrate what she has learned in life, implementing the best of the best, so that you reap the benefits.

She continues to learn and is a member of many international training groups, mastermind communities and forums. Perhaps, a little obsessive with her drive to know more.

Although this is primarily a book about dogs, her work with horses has helped her enormously with this journey. Whether horse, dog or human we have so much in common. We can connect on so many levels. Perhaps, like Sonia, you will want to dig a bit deeper? Learn more and do better?

After reading this book and implementing the strategies, you will be able to have a wonderful, well-behaved canine companion. You will gain the confidence to know that he is safe, calm and happy, living the best life with you. No more stress and arguments blamed on the dog. You'll finally have that great quality time with your dog with pleasant, therapeutic walks, and much more time for your busy life or socialising with friends and family. Say goodbye to the frustration and embarrassment.

Currently we have sixteen rescue huskies or husky crosses, two Jack Russells and two nine-week-old Golden Retriever pups. The majority live in the house, with some huskies choosing to live in the paddock (with shelter of course). We intend to train the pups for service work for people with special needs. Sonia has done similar work in the past mainly with horses. We operate the business from home so always have clients calling, many with young children and their own dogs. Many of our clients have special needs. Lexie and Sonia work from home together with one part time staff member. The business is non-profit making dedicated to the rescue of huskies.

We understand the need to balance your busy life, your responsibilities and time spent with Fido. We are full time carers for a family member with severe Alzheimer's, together with another family member who is registered disabled. Sonia has raised a large family and now has grandchildren.

Lexie is working towards a BA degree in Management and Leadership (chartered) and has worked in the family husky and dog training business for 5 years. She has been surrounded by horses and dogs all her life. Lexie has the IT, media and technical skills necessary to today's successful business.

We use all the principles given in this book to keep everybody safe, calm, happy and have a peaceful household. Huskies are known to be a challenging breed, not the easiest to train, yet this approach works for them too. Even if they are a rescue. Two of the huskies have had twelve homes in six months, they were one day away from being euthanised, and now they live full and productive lives. Though, it's true that we did need to raise our game (and our fences) for these Harry Houdini Hooligans. They are now settled, happy and enjoy their life.

At the beginning of each chapter you will read a testimonial. We had difficulty in choosing which to use. Within each chapter we will name our example dog after the testimonial study. Towards the end of each chapter there will be a brief case study showing the steps we took to achieve the transformation of the example dog from being deviant to becoming a dream so that you can see the process in action.

After you have read the book, if you implement the four principles and strategies and have fun together playing the games, you will see a complete transformation in your partnership, your household and your walks. You will have all that you need to address any struggle you have been experiencing with Fido.

You will also find you are using the knowledge and skills in your everyday life, not just with your dog. You will experience a fundamental shift in your thinking towards a more positive mindset, one that looks for creative solutions and is more flexible. This can become a way of life.

Our ultimate aim, or 'powerful why', is to provide you with the knowledge, motivation and mindset for you to transform your dog into the dog of your dreams; avoiding adding to the frightening statistics of rescue dogs.

DEVIANT DOG TO DREAM DOG
THE FOUR PRINCIPLES FOR TRANSFORMATION

DISCOVER THE DOG OF YOUR DREAMS INSIDE THE ONE YOU ALREADY HAVE.

PART 1

THE DOG END
OF THE LEASH

1.1

YOUR DOG'S NATURE
THE DOGGYNESS OF A DOG.

CHAPTER INTRODUCTION:

The Seven Emotional Systems that drive Patch
to action and determine his decisions:

- SEEKING
- RAGE
- FEAR
- LUST
- CARE
- PANIC
- PLAY

A brief testimonial of Patch, a Male Collie/Beagle cross:

"I loved learning about a dog's needs, especially how seeking the food was so rewarding. I found that once I understood that Patch, my Collie/Beagle cross was over-threshold and just couldn't think when he was shouting and screaming at other dogs. It wasn't just that he was being naughty or stubborn, which helped me when I became annoyed with him.

As it happened, he had separation anxiety and this information helped me to understand life from his point of view. Following the advice, which included information on holistic treatment, he is making huge progress. I realised, among other mistakes, that although I thought I was only asking for small increases in time home alone I had not broken it down enough, I was not taking baby steps but adult strides which were just too much for him to deal with."

We made the decision to share the information in this chapter because, although it can seem a little 'deep', 'nerdy' or going into unnecessary details, we believe that when we know the reason behind the behaviour of the animal, we find the struggle. It helps us to be more patient, and creative with our solutions, no matter how extreme or crazy they may seem to others.

It is knowledge that can make the difference between you assuming Patch is stubborn or naughty and realising that they are struggling too. Patch may likely be experiencing high levels of stress and finding it difficult to cope with life in our human world.

If your dog's emotional state is too intense, he will not be able to learn, the neural pathways for thinking are not connected at that moment. We need to recognise this emotional state so we can adapt our own behaviour for a more positive and constructive interaction

Science Alert:

<u>The seven needs (drives) and how they apply to dogs.</u>

We are constantly projecting our emotions onto our dogs, but what is really going on? Do they feel similar emotions to us or are we simply imagining it?

Panksepp et al identified 7 emotional systems that he termed 'SEEKING', 'RAGE', 'FEAR', 'LUST', 'CARE', 'PANIC' AND 'PLAY'. These emotions are buried deep within the sub cortical (primitive) areas of the brain. These areas are similar across all mammals – including humans. We have the same basic structures and systems as our dogs.

Emotions are a feedback system that tell us if various stimulation is positive/pleasant or negative/unpleasant. Whether something is experienced as a reinforcer (something good) or a punisher. Therefore, how an animal feels about a situation will greatly depend on the feedback – it will be either a good or bad depending on the emotion felt.

For example, a dog worried about strangers would likely experience negative or worrying emotions if it were to be petted by them. While, if the owner pets them, and they have a good relationship, then this is seen as a positive experience.

The same act of a human patting the dog is interpreted in a completely different way: a good thing or a scary, negative, punishing thing. The action is identical, but the effect is very different.

Following on from this, if you have a dog (maybe a recent rescue) that is showing anxiety, it is best not to assume that you stroking it (no matter how compassionately with all the best intentions) will be helpful to the dog. You may be inadvertently adding to their stress.

An animal's emotions are the basis of thought. Emotion guides, motivates and attracts attention. For instance, the Seeking emotion drives Patch to hunt for the toy or food. Emotions drive us all to action and determine our decisions.

However, it is important to note that humans do have a larger neo cortex which process emotions into more elaborate emotions like shame or guilt. Many people do believe animals feel guilt because they look guilty; won't make eye contact, have a body language that to many humans' projects shame or guilt.

In reality, it is most likely that Patch knows the human is mad and that, in similar situations, they may have shouted at and/or punished Patch. What Patch may actually be doing is trying to appease their human by being submissive to avoid punishment. This often works to minimise negative actions from the human, so to them it's definitely worth doing again whenever the human is in a bad mood.

> Maybe next time you are in a bad mood, check Patch's behaviour? What is his response to your mood? Does he show the same 'guilty' expression?

Both humans and animals are emotionally driven. We need to recognise what emotional state Patch is in so we can adapt our own behaviour for a more positive and constructive interaction. It is incredibly important for us to take responsibility for our own emotions and understand how they affect our reactions and the subsequent behaviour of our pets.

We expect our dogs to have self-control and not follow their needs when we don't wish it. However, we are often not prepared to practice self-control ourselves. We can be less than honest about our own emotions. The first stage for our self-control is to be able to recognise our own emotions and acknowledge how we feel. We need to be more self-aware. This takes time and will help us in all other aspects of our life – not just our dog training. More detail on how we can control our emotions, frustrations will be in later chapters. In Chapter 4.1 we talk about effectively communicating with our companions and dealing with frustration especially. This is the fourth principle, the human end of the leash.

<u>Diving into Patch's emotional systems:</u>

The SEEKING System

This is an incredibly important system which underlies so many of Patch's be- haviours. If a task is enjoyable then he will feel pleasure from the activity; This is down to a release of dopamine, a 'feel-good' chemical. In a dog bred for herding, stalking, chasing or running then these activities release the pleasure chemical, this can be addictive. Think about how Patch may seem obsessive to you about chasing a ball, a bike or anything else that moves. For example, Patch, a Collie/Beagle cross, may be more prone to this behaviour due to his breeding where collies are made to chase and beagles No matter the breed, this can always be managed.

When dogs are prevented from performing the activities they have been hardwired (in their DNA) to do then they will often redirect their behaviour into another activity that is generally unwanted by their owner such as chasing bikes or cars.

Some of these behaviours can seem very strange and initially began as a coping mechanism which has now become a habit. Examples include spinning or biting the wheels of cars or bikes. Repeated behaviour sequences that to our minds seem like obsessive, compulsive behaviour or just plain weird.

If Patch is exhibiting strange (to you) behaviour, consider which emotion he is feeling. What behaviour does he really want to express? Consider how he is being blocked from doing what he feels he is driven to by his genes and doggyness to do.

The RAGE System

When the Seeking system is switched on, but is not satisfied, then Patch might become angry and show rage. This may be if he wants to chase something or greet another dog but is prevented etc. Thus, Patch, in a very over excited state may show anger and, perhaps, bite the person or dog next to him. If Patch is very hungry and prevented from eating then, again, Rage may result.

If Patch is feeling pain or irritated, Rage can result. Pain can be a common factor in changing the behaviour of your dog. A previously placid and calm animal may suddenly show different (perhaps unacceptable to you) behaviour. Patch may growl or bite, or perhaps show increased reactivity. Therefore, any sudden change in the behaviour and personality of Patch needs investigating. Probably the first port of call will be your vet or dog expert. If you have rescued or rehomed Patch, you may be able to contact the previous foster home or shelter/dog home for more information.

The CARE System

This is critical for the survival of any offspring: the mother will run to her pups when she hears their distress call. The care system includes the maternal behaviour of allowing the pups to suckle, being calm and patient with them, cleaning them and cleaning up after them. This behaviour is very much controlled by hormones.

This system is triggered by hormonal changes, but it also involves the bond that animals develop for other animals and of course, us. The bonding between us and Patch involves this caring system. For example, oxytocin (a reproductive hormone) is released by both our dog and the human when we sit close or look into each other's eyes. The more often this is done the more we are likely to have a great bond and feel good in each other's company.

The Care system and its link with the Rage system: Very importantly (especially with rescue dogs) lack of acceptance, and love, restrictions from rights and pleasure, abuse or neglect can damage the dog and lead to long term anger. This is a hugely important topic which I will return to. This is an area where often we try to make up for the previous lack of. Be it real or perceived. Nevertheless, we must be careful about how we proceed. Again, our intentions may be good, but we may need more knowledge and skill to know how best we can help.

Patch feels more than one emotion at any one time. We will explore this in more depth in later chapters. For now, consider fear. It can trigger a defensive action for example, biting and is actually a more common cause than Rage. It can be that intense fear coupled with over excitement (arousal) leads to Rage.

The FEAR System

Science tells us that there are three neural pathways that are involved in the fear response.

1. The High Road: Patch is still able to make decisions; he may be able to think if the fear is not too intense. Good training and preparation can assist in this. The example of this pathway would be if Patch were to hear a sudden noise, the information would be sent to the sensory cortex where the information is processed. Patch then makes a decision for the

best action to be safe and behaves accordingly. In this case, he may bark.

This can explain when dogs labelled as reactive (barking and lunging) who, when in the presence of lots of dogs all off-leash together may not show their previous reactive behaviour.

To be barking and lunging in this situation is not likely to be safe amidst so many other dogs. Whereas Patch seeing only one other dog on a leash in the distance shows the reactive behaviour. In one situation he makes a decision to behave in one way to keep safe but in the other he behaves completely differently.

> *Note: This can be very confusing to the owner as Patch has been given the label of reactive when he sees other dogs but is not always reactive. We then are likely giving Patch the further label of him being unpredictable. The seemingly 'unpredictable' nature of a dog will also be explored later in the book. Once we know more, we realise that it is, in fact, predictable.*

2. The Low Road: Patch makes no decisions; he is no longer thinking. This pathway is formed from memory of previous situations so goes from thalamus to amygdala. This is an emergency response with no thinking involved.

> *In this situation the dog may well get into trouble and put himself in danger. This may be the reason for Patch running out in front of a car when hearing a loud bang. He may even jump through a window to escape a scary situation.*

3. Stress Road: Neural pathways are established as previously stressful situations are experienced. Patch is not thinking. In high stress condition he is incapable of thought and cannot learn. This route is between the amygdala and periaqueductal grey of the brain. Patch will anticipate and try to avoid the situation. This can often be the basis of anxiety disorders.

We can see from the above that there is a physiology of neural pathways and chemicals involved. This makes changing the behaviour more challenging for us. That's not to say that it isn't doable, however.

The LUST System

It will be no surprise to anyone as to how powerful a motivator the effects of hormones can be. Animals will go without food or stay in exposed conditions in extreme discomfort in order to mate. These strong urges are clearly important to the survival of the species. The sexual drive can change Patch's behaviour to such an extent that they do not seem like the same dog. We may need to work very hard to be able to keep our dog's cooperation in the face of these hormonal rampages.

Rest assured we can help Patch through these hormonal periods. Many rescue centres have already neutered the dogs in their care before rehoming, or it may be a condition that the new home does so.

Important Advice: Please be aware that early spaying and castration does carry health and behavioural risks as indeed does neutering later in life. Hormones are there for a reason and are integral to healthy function. Many vets are keen to encourage neutering, being cynical why wouldn't they? Thankfully, more and more vets are taking another view and helping the owner to a more informed choice.

Before rushing out and neutering your companion, conduct your own research so that you can make the best decision for you, your lifestyle and your pet.

The PANIC System

Many dogs are said to have separation anxiety when they may in fact be feeling a milder level of emotion. True separation anxiety is a tough nut to crack. Milder versions can still be challenging but with a step by step, holistic approach we can expect a successful outcome.

Many mammal species show emotional pain when they are separated. This may be a survival strategy that they are safer when in a group or herd. When separated, animals are more exposed to danger.

Interestingly, the areas in the brain that regulate this system overlaps with areas responsible for physical pain. This suggests that separation can trigger very distressing emotional reaction, such as a panic attack.

Patch can cause a great deal of harm to himself and his environment under such intense emotion. Remember Patch cannot think under such stressful conditions. Be aware that when Patch tears up the couch or chews through a door, he is experiencing real fear. It is very painful for him. He cannot think or learn under such circumstances and needs help.

When it comes to rehomed animals, it is especially sad when they damage the home and the new owners feel that they cannot remain. In this case they may well be rehomed yet again which adds to their stress.

The PLAY System

Play is incredibly important in animals as it promotes a more relaxed and happy state of mind. It is essential that we never underestimate the importance of this system. Play facilitates social attachments and improves social skills. The play system involves the release of endorphins or other opioids which result in a euphoric state of mind.

Research in both the animal and human world has shown that just seven or eight repetitions of an act can result in learning when play is involved rather than up to four hundred drill type repetitions.

It is clear with such research that the best option is to use games to help Patch learn the skills we want him to, rather than repeating the action for hundreds of times in the hopes that it will eventually sink in. Transformations can be made incredibly quickly by harnessing the power of play and utilising games. Several games are introduced and discussed in Section 2 and 3.

A Brief Case Study

Patch was a very high energy, nervous guy. His owners had reached a point where they believed they would have to rehome him. They were unable to leave him at home and him be settled and calm. He needed his human 'mum' who was primarily at home with him but there were times they wanted to be able to leave him. This is not the place to discuss Separation Anxiety in great detail, all you need to know is that it is not an easy fix.

By keeping Patch under threshold, using the calming protocol, to gradually increasing duration on a boundary with her owner being absent huge improvements have been gained. We ditched the routine, so Patch did not have cues which made him anticipate his mum leaving. We ditched the bowl, so the daily allowance of food was used to build a love of the boundary. We also used calming games such as scatter feeding, ninja feeding and lots of scent work. The scent work really appealed to his beagle drive to sniff and hunt.

Patch was on medication from the vet when we met, but by only taking small baby steps, utilising calming herbs and aromatherapy oils (with the vet's knowledge) he can now be perfectly happy home alone. Patch is now prescribed medication free. He actively chooses the aromatherapy scents he prefers (this does vary). He seems to enjoy listening to soothing classical music. His owners choose to continue with the oils and music.

Calming massages were used to help Patch relax and meet his need for touch/care drive. We also worked on games to increase his confidence. Optimism, flexibility and tolerance of frustration.

Options such as getting another dog for a companion were discussed but, given that the separation anxiety was for a specific human (mum), it would not be likely that another dog would have helped. We do like dogs to have a dog friend in the household, remember they are social beings. Although it's not always possible, Patch's owners preferred to stay with a single dog.

Summary

- The knowledge that our dogs and ourselves are emotionally wired in much the same way can help us to understand that they have strong needs and drives. This gives us some insight into why our previous training methods may not be working. For example, we can get recall at home but not in more distracting environments.

- The seven emotional systems identified by Panksepp et al: SEEKING, RAGE, FEAR, LUST, CARE, PANIC and PLAY will influence how your dog feels about a situation: as a good thing or a bad thing depending on previous experience and genes.

- Emotions are the basis of thought, emotions guide, motivates and gets ours and Patch's attention. Emotions drive us to action and determines our decisions.

- Please remember it is hard to be a dog in our human world, to have the self-control we desire or expect and not follow doggie instincts and drives. Patch cannot learn when stressed and over threshold, he is not being naughty he is emotionally struggling. He needs help.

Mythbuster Moment: When Patch is being naughty or stubborn etc. He knows he has been bad because he is acting guilty. Patch is not, in actuality, looking guilty he is simply using appeasement behaviour to avoid punishment. He has noted your bad mood and remembers what has happened in similar circumstances and is trying to not be hurt.

In the next chapter we will dig deeper into these core emotions and explore their effect.

THE POWER OF EMOTIONS

CHAPTER INTRODUCTION:

How emotions impact on motivation and behaviour.

When it comes to our dogs, you are already the expert.
As your relationship progresses you will become more and more
practiced and confident in identifying their mood state.

We must never underestimate the power of
emotions as a driving force. For example:

- Too much early stress (even in the womb) may have long term negative effects.
- Touch can release 'feel good' chemicals providing your dog is comfortable with it.
- Play is necessary for good neural growth and brain maturity. A third of your dog's genes are modified by play.
- Seeking (or foraging) also releases 'feel good' chemicals. Enrichment activities help ensure the seeking drive is met.

A brief testimonial of Molly, a female Poodle/Maltese cross:

"Learning to pay attention to Molly's emotional state, being willing to change my plans and just being flexible when it comes to her, has helped her enormously. I once thought that she simply needed to get used to things and hoped her reactivity would reduce. It didn't, it got worse.

I found she really enjoyed gentle handling, learning some basic massage techniques and simply relaxing together especially before we went out worked miracles. I especially use this if I see her starting to tense up, I am getting much better at reading her body language. I can also keep her from starting to worry by playing some fun games. It is lovely when she tells me she wants to play, or if she wants a cuddle. She's so very different from the bundle of nerves she used to be."

Whatever emotion your dog is feeling be it anger, fear or loneliness pay attention to it. Note it, consider it and take appropriate action. We will be getting to appropriate actions later. You are already Molly's expert and will become more and more practiced and confident in spotting her mood state. You are her advocate. Her voice in our human world.

Dogs show core emotions which influence their brain, behaviour and welfare. Never underestimate the power of emotions as a driving force.

The good news is we can influence their emotions, and therefore their motivation, and behaviour. No matter the breed, age of the dog or even its previous experiences we can work towards, and achieve, our goals as well as the behaviour we do want.

In this integrative approach we will be utilising the powerful emotions to gain the behaviour we do want; we will learn how to avoid and minimise the emotions that cause us to become stuck in our training.

The power of the emotions of GRIEF and CARE (Love).

Grief and Care are the foundation of the social bonding system, friendship and parents. Lots of time is spend in body contact or close to someone. When young animals feel lonely, they become agitated. Lonely young social animals will be loud and active and in a panicky state. Grief activates the Caring System in the adults when their young is panicking and agitated. The young shouts and the parent responds.

Grief caused by separation lights up the brain more than any other emotion. Many animals may die from separation depression. Different chemicals lead to depression. However, we cannot spoil young animals by too much care, while we will not make them needy and spoilt as is commonly believed, the effects of social interactions early on have a long-term effect.

In a dangerous environment it pays to be cautious; to be a little fearful has survival benefits. If in a safe environment then the bold, confident animal is most successful. Animals are risk takers and do enjoy the adrenaline buzz – up to a point. It is the bold, confident personality that thrives in our busy and complex human world.

It is important to note that a mum who has experienced a great deal of stress whilst pregnant passes on the effects to the pups. The stress hormones in her body pass through to the pups who develop with too many stress hormones. This affects their growth, welfare and personality. Pups will then pass on the potential issues to their pups. This implications of this for puppy farming and the stress the dog feels during pregnancy are clear.

Knowing this fact can help us understand the fact that when buying from unknown breeders, or taking dogs from shelters, we do not know their stress history.

An animal whose nature means they are easily stressed may not bond as readily with humans, in such a case it can be difficult to help the dog to become calm, confident and secure. Fortunately, there are techniques, skills and baby steps that can be used to help shape the personality of any dog, no matter their breed or age.

The role of touch in shaping Molly's personality, helping change her emotions, motivation and behaviour:

One major key to shaping personality is touch. Gentle touch releases oxytocin and endorphins, activating the Parasympathetic Nervous System. This lowers blood pressure, heart rate and leads to deeper breathing and relaxation.

The benefits of us stroking, massaging and gentle touches on the dog will help the bonding process and activate the Caring system's emotional response. This has the integral 'feel good' factor for our dog (and us).

> Note: Not all dogs are ready to be cuddled, handled etc. We may need to take another approach until they signal their readiness to engage with us. We must never assume the dog's readiness when it comes to handling them.

Studies into Hugging:

Studies show that when being hugged 80% of dogs show discomfort.

Humans, on the other hand, like hugging and we feel good when we hug. Dogs do not hug nor is it in their behaviour repertoire. We need to read Molly's body language. Children do hug very tightly, it is safer if they do not hug Molly, especially if they also like to press their faces up to Molly's face. If she cannot move away, she may feel trapped, become fearful which may leash to a behaviour you do not want. If she is told off for growling, she may feel she needs to nip.

To gain insight into where your Molly may like to be touched consider:

1. Where do dogs normally groom or touch each other?
2. What does it look like?

Try to mimic these behaviours where you feel appropriate. It is often scent marking glands where they groom each other.

How do we know if Molly is enjoying our touch?

You often tell you companion appreciates your touch when they nudge your hand back or follow your hand with their body when your remove it. By doing this they clearly show they wish to reinitiate contact. They are giving you permission. You can assume they are enjoying it. If they move away, simply stop the touch. It is important we pay attention to the consent that they provide us.

> Note: You may feel good when hugging and stroking Molly because you are getting an oxytocin and endorphin fix. Molly, on the other hand, may be feeling stressed. She may be able to be stroked in one context but not another.

Some animals, those fearful and distrustful, could be dangerous to initiate the contact by touch. We may, in fact, make them so uncomfortable that they bite. If this is the case, we can use other strategies to develop a great relationship with Molly. Once we build the trust and respect, often Molly feels comfortable with touch.

Utilising PLAY to switch emotions:

When using play, we can switch negative anxiety to a positive mind set. This will have a powerful effect on behaviour.

Try engaging Molly with a toy or food. Food can switch them from the sympathetic nervous system which is responsible for the 'on switch' of the fight or flight response (RAGE or FEAR) to the parasympathetic nervous system, which is the 'off switch'.

Having fun and playing with a toy can switch the emotion which has a powerful effect on behaviour. Molly may then initiate the contact, so she is in control of the interaction. She chooses to come close to play and becomes more comfortable with the proximity, perhaps even putting her paws on you. Casual, fleeting touches are often then accepted. We can build from there. Play and fear are opposites, Molly can learn not to fear the scary things; As long as Molly is not too fearful, you can use play to inhibit fear.

Play is a core emotion which affects mood, confidence and welfare. It promotes social bonding, which can be within or between species. This means when you play with Molly, she is more likely to seek you out in the future.

Animals that are able to play are less fearful, less aggressive. Play promotes the understanding of, cooperation and compassion for others. If play is unavailable Molly can become more irritable. Molly is likely to prefer places where she has played in the past.

Molly will prefer to be in the company of someone who plays and is generally happy. An interesting study with rats initially demonstrated this; Young rats chose to be in the company of rats who were in a good mood and avoided the bad mood (grumpy, irritable) rats. For Molly to want to seek you out, exhibit a happy mood and play games.

The brain matures by play, the cortex undergoes many changes, neural growth factors are activated and a third of the genes are modified by play. It can even help Molly to recover from a poor start or traumatic experiences

Play impacts positively on the brain, we can turn a bad relationship/ memory around by the repeated positive interactions of play.

Play can be used before and during more serious training sessions. The level of excitement can be controlled through play and it can be used as reinforcement. It has real life, quick, powerful, positive results.

Utilising the SEEKING system.

Seeking is a foraging behaviour. It means exploring and making decisions for the dog. The anticipation of the food, the seeking and the chase is the true reinforcing and fun factor. Once they have the food, their fun  ends. The hunt for food is far more entertaining for the dog over simply being given it. Playing games for Molly to seek out her food will result in a very enriching life.

The heart of the seeking system is the dopamine in the amygdala. This dopamine rush is reinforcing, and Molly will work hard to get the 'feel good' factor of this release. The dopamine rush is diminished when eating where the parasympathetic system takes over. This system is also responsible for digestion.

Unwanted behaviour is often a result of under-stimulation. Seeking may result in Molly getting into trouble. Given the fact that it is a core emotion, various triggers in the environment can stimulate the seeking response. To help prevent this, we must provide plenty of opportunity to satisfy Molly's needs in a manner than we are comfortable with.

Clicker training is an example of utilising the seeking system, thus allows Molly to satisfy her seeking needs. Animals are very keen and enjoy the dopamine surge that comes with anticipating the reward (seeking the reward). By using treats and using a mechanical noise maker such as a 'clicker', the sound becomes a reward in itself. It is the pairing of the click and the reward. This allows you to use the click independently to act in place of a reward.

Understanding is the first step to change. There is likely to be a shift in how you interact with animals because of how you perceive animals.

A Brief Case Study

Molly was a very high energy and anxious dog. She found it difficult to rest and relax. She was described by her owners as very reactive to just about everything. She would bark, lunge and spin when she saw other dogs from even long distances. She would lunge at cars and bikes. Her owners described taking her on walks to be very embarrassing and frustrating. They tried to reassure and calm her but found that it did not seem to make a difference. She would continue to lunge, spin and bark. They had been to four other trainers but did not seem to make progress.

Molly also barked at home, out of the windows as people walked by, charged the fencing outside to bark at passers-by. If she was out in the garden, she would bark at the neighbours if they were in their garden.

Molly spent the majority of the time with her stress bucket overflowing so she could not learn a new way to respond. She spent a lot of her time barking and being over vigilant. Enrichment and calming activities were put in place. Scent games and lots of brain games to help her use her seeking drive. We made use of calming boundary games and the calmness protocol.

No walks for several weeks so she did not rehearse the lunging, barking and spinning behaviour instead all the games were played inside the house, then in the garden when it was quiet, and no neighbours were in their garden. If a neighbour came out Molly was on a long line and simply taken inside using games such as all eyes on me and treats from the sky. The main thing was to prevent the rehearsal of the behaviour that was not wanted and to replace it with calm behaviour, playing games.

To prevent the jumping up at the windows and barking at passers-by, blinds were drawn and Molly spent more time at the back of the house where she could not see the people therefore was not triggered to bark. Molly was not left out in the garden, so she did not spend her time barking, rehearsing the behaviour that was not wanted. Quiet times of the day were chosen to play the games outside. Molly remained on a long line as her recall was not likely to be good if she was fence running. As Molly became more focussed with the games and her owners more skilful with their mechanics in delivering the food or toy, she was able to play them in the garden even with distractions of people walking by.

Molly's owners became more skilful at reading her body language and being able to judge when she was relaxed and able to stay focused on the games. Molly was driven out to a quiet location, more games played and taken home.

Molly enjoyed being massaged with a loving gentle, soothing touch. Her owners can now see when she starts to tense and can offer a massage. They have noticed she is able to relax and sleep well afterwards. By keeping Molly's bucket empty and her being able to relax, Molly was able to learn she had more fun playing the games with her owners, she gained in confidence, was no longer over-excited so did not feel the need to bark, spin and lunge. She discovered new ways to behave as she could remain calm.

Molly can now be in the garden with the neighbours out in their garden, she chooses to remain on a boundary in the garden with a Kong, scatter feed or play games. Management is in place she is not out unattended.

She is encouraged to rest and sleep by spending time in her covered crate in a quiet room. This ensures her stress bucket stays well below threshold.

By playing the whole range of games Molly now has a bigger stress bucket with bigger hole so if she does go over threshold, she is able to calm down much more quickly.

Her owners know that if they have a blip, perhaps they have left her outside for a while by mistake, or they had not noticed a dog nearby and Molly reacts, they ensure she spends a day or two resting at home, playing calming games to reset.

It eases their stress to know they have the tools and strategies. They have seen huge improvements and see Molly is so much more relaxed, safe, calm and happy.

Summary

- In this chapter we have explored how we can start to enrich Molly's life by giving her opportunities to do some of her natural doggie behaviour, for her emotional drives to be met. We will show you how you can further meet Molly's needs in the chapters following.
- The power of touch is very strong, helping to meet the care system needs.
- We discussed how play can help switch into a positive emotional state. The role of play and seeking has been explored and we will be digging much deeper in the following chapters.

Mythbuster Moment: Dogs don't actually like to be hugged, watch closely, maybe try videoing Molly having a hug, check out the Body Language chapter of this book and judge if Molly is happy having a hug. In studies, 80% of dogs showed they were uncomfortable with hugging. Children do tend to hug very tightly, if Molly cannot move away then she may feel she needs to escalate in her behaviour.

THE IMPORTANCE OF CALMNESS

CHAPTER INTRODUCTION:

How to keep your dog safe, calm and happy.

- The importance of 'stress buckets', how going 'over-threshold' is likely to adversely affect behaviour.
- Arousal plus valence, or chemical bond, equals emotion.
- 'Happy land' and 'Sad land'; How being in 'Sad Land' while adding Excitement spells trouble ahead.
- Tolerance of frustration depending on a dog's past and personality.
- Practiced behaviour becoming repeated behaviour.
- The Calmness Circle: calming activities, the calmness procedure and rest.
- The circle of emotions.
- The excitement table.
- Calmness over the day: How 90-95% of the day should be calm. A dog only needs 5-10% of positive high excitement activity. (E.g. 30 minutes.)
- Yerkes-Dodson Law: Arousal and performance. Performance increases with arousal, however too much arousal makes performance decline.

A brief testimonial of Bob, a male Border Collie:

"Bob my border collie was very hyper and could not settle at all. I realised after a coaching session with Sonia that he was not having enough opportunity to sleep and rest. His stress bucket was always full. We implemented a new regime to ensure at least 18 hours sleep and rest time. We avoided high excitement activities for three days by staying at home and doing calming games. The result was amazing; we have a different dog. He is so much happier and so are we. We have the confidence to make a start on other aspects of his behaviour, we can already see improvement. He listens to us now."

A great deal of our learning has come from the study of psychology, but also from the world of ethology (the study of animals in their natural environment). As was pointed out in the first chapter, the physiology behind human emotions and animal emotions is essentially the same: Both in terms of the neural connections (parts of the brain) and the neurochemicals (within the body) involved. Essentially this means that our fight or flight response is the same as Bobs.

The graphs and diagrams in this chapter are taken from a mixture of human and animal research. Rest assured they apply equally to each. As you will discover social animals such as dogs have much in common with us.

Here is a question for you: On the one side you have Bob who is screaming, lunging and spinning when he sees another dog. On the other, you have Rover who is licking his lips, trembling, tries to turn around and avoids the other dog.

The question is which of the two dogs above is most fearful? Which one will be most difficult to train to be comfortable with seeing another dog?

The answer: There is no way of knowing from their behaviour.

The chosen behaviour does not relate to the intensity of the emotion felt. A dog that is licking his lips and moving slowly may in fact be experiencing considerable stress equal or more than the one exhibiting the more extreme behaviour.

> Note: Much of the information you may have previously learned of behaviour signs and how to read your dog's body language are over simplified and easy to misinterpret. It is hard to know the emotion that Bob is experiencing by just reading his body language.

What we do know is that whether Bob is experiencing rage or fear, we need to help him become calm and happy.One idea that may help you to understand is to consider each behaviour as coming out of a particular box for over arousal behaviour. As below, each of these behaviours can be clues that Bob is overly aroused.

Examples of the clues of over-arousal:		
Barking	Howling	Growling
Hiding	Escaping	Pulling on leash
Lagging on leash	Chasing	Trembling/Shaking
Being restless	Pacing	Being vigilant
Circling	Seeking out people	Increasing owner attachment
Salivating	Lip licking	Panting
A stronger/harder mouth when taking treats	Cheek puffing	Yawning
Staring	Ground sniffing	Self-grooming
Scratching	Agression	Leash lunging
Biting leash	Playing, aggressing or staring at invisible things	Unresponsiveness
Freezing	Disinterest in treats that are normally enjoyed	Inability to respond to learnt cues

We need now to introduce you to a word you may not have come across: Valence. Valence, in our case, is a means of determining whether something is interpreted by the animal as good or bad, positive or negative. Positive Valence emotions include excitement, happiness and calmness in descending level of arousal felt.

Negative valence emotions would be fear, anxiety, worry and uneasiness. Again, in descending level of arousal.

Arousal + Valence = Emotion

Using this formula, we can create our excitement table as shown in the figure below. When it comes to emotions, dogs can be in any one of these sections.

	Negative Valence (Sad Land)	Positive Valence (Happy Land)
High Arousal	Fear	Excitement
Low Arousal	Anxiety	Calmness

It is powerful when you understand this; It helps you to predict the emotion that will result from a particular situation or context. Whereas previously you may have believed Bob to be unpredictable you will now see that, as you gain knowledge, you become more attuned to reading Bob's body language. When you pay attention, you will be able to predict what is likely to happen and understand just why it happened. Better still, you will become more proactive and able to intervene to prevent a negative interaction.

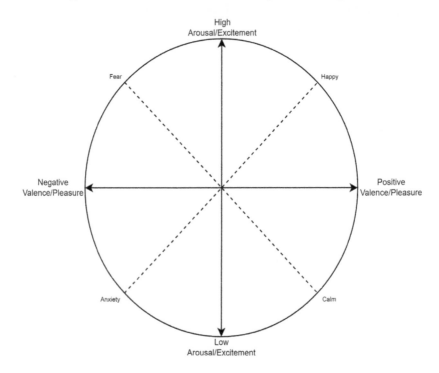

Imagine the scene where you have just had a game of tug with Bob (high excitement/arousal) and a barking dog approaches. The barking dog provides a negative valence which makes Bob become fearful.

Negative Valence of barking dog + Excitement/Arousal = Fear

Now, in the next situation, we have a calm and happy Bob. The approach of the barking dog is now only low-level negative valence. In this case, it is easy to switch back into the calm and happy mood once the barking dog is out of sight.

(Low Level Negative Valence) + (Low Excitement /Arousal) + (Positive, Calming Activity) = (Calmness)

To help a Bob who has just switched into a fear state, you need to reduce the arousal/excitement and add positive valence/outcomes. In later chapters I will go into more detail and give techniques and games to play to help you do this. These games will give you real life results, very quickly.

You can see how important it is to keep Bob in happy land on the positive side of the circle.

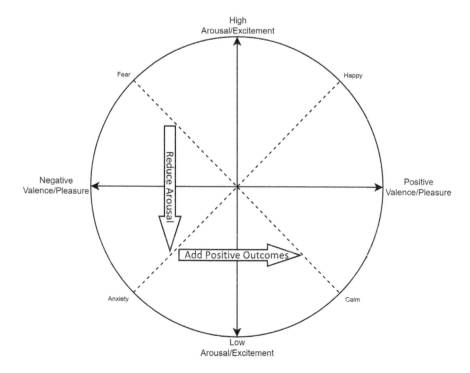

Now, instead of reactivity, we will move on to actively increasing Bob's performance. Let's say we wanted Bob to do a difficult agility course. To do this, we use our Positive Valence, or Happy Land, and we add some excitement. It's important that we do not do this for too long before he attempts the course. Short, fun play sessions will help to raise the testosterone levels (even for females). This lifts Bob's confidence. But, if we play for too long, then the stress hormone (Cortisol) keeps raising and their testosterone level falls which leads to them feeling stress.

This brings us onto frustration. When Bob anticipates something, but it doesn't happen, then frustration may be felt (let's be honest, it's the same for us humans!). This anticipation could be anything such as Bob wanting to greet a person or dog across the road to waiting for his meal or walkies. All of these can cause Bob frustration should he be blocked from his goal.

> It is important to realise that the behaviour Bob exhibits whilst feeling frustrated may be identical to those when he is fearful, worried or over-excited. The ability to deal with frustration without barking, lunging, spinning etc. will make life so much happier for all. This is something that can be achieved by playing the games later in the book.

Teaching Bob the ability to tolerate frustration is something that is vital to him becoming more resilient to changes in his environment and it creates a learner who is more robust to mistakes made by their partner. Not only that, but it enhances his learning ability. Because Bob can now cope with failure, he will try harder instead.

Think of a situation where you were frustrated and gave up. Now think of a situation where you were frustrated but tried harder and succeeded.

The more we can view 'failure' as an opportunity to learn, the more we can cope with the frustration of the situation. In the end we can simply change tactics and try again.

> Both partners need to learn the ability to cope with frustration. Change tactics if something isn't working for you. Perhaps approach the problem in a different way, manage your environment and try again. Maybe consider attempting it on another day when the mood is right.
>
> We are all social animals, so remember that what applies to Bob also applies to you.

Additionally, when dealing with frustration, we must take into consideration Bob's life. For example, many rescue dogs may have a poor tolerance. This can show up as a number of things:

- Being completely off-balance by even the smallest of changes in their routine.
- Bob failing to think through a struggle and simply stops trying.
- Bob not trying new choices, only repeating the same response that is not achieving the reward. At some point he will give up all together.
- Bob may do other random behaviour such as sniffing, biting or zoomies. He may disengage from the training completely and do other doggy behaviour instead.

> Note: It is possible that dogs being thrown off-balance by a change in routine is the reason why the common advice is for dogs to have a fixed routine. However, sometimes life happens. Perhaps someone else must take over and they have their own routine that the dog is not used to. This can result in severe stress for a dog that has poor tolerance. While initially we may have some routine, we are best to remove it. This creates a greater flexibility and the ability to cope with frustration in the future. This can be done in baby steps. We don't have to ditch all the routines all at once. We must consider our dog's personality; we should remember that all are individuals who can go at difference paces.

One common problem we have with our companions is their reactivity when it comes to other dogs. A likely cause of this would be the prevention of allowing Bob to meet the other dog. This triggers the feeling of frustration, adding Negative Valence into the equation. Coupling this with high excitement results in fear. This fearful emotion becomes associated in Bob's mind with seeing another dog. This leads to fear-based reactivity.

Similarly, the frustration behaviours such as Bob circling and barking, may lead to the other dog, let's call her Fifi, being worried. Fifi may then react, which ends up with both dogs exhibiting these behaviours, escalating the situation. This is remembered as a pattern of behaviour and may be repeated next time.

> *Any behaviour once practiced is highly likely to be repeated. Essentially this is how Bob has learned to deal with the situation, and as far as he was concerned, it worked. He kept himself safe, made the other dog go away, and kept a distance plus it helped him feel better to actively do something (bark and leap around) to cope with his emotions.*

One hugely interesting piece of research is that dogs who showed high levels of active stress related behaviour when separated from their friends, shouting, screaming, destroying furniture, trashing the house actually had lower levels of stress hormones than other dogs who were unhappy being separated from their friends, but chose to lie quietly.

This does mean we need to be aware that Bob, who is quiet upon being left, is not necessarily happy or comfortable. But, don't worry we're not saying you cannot leave Bob alone at all. What we are saying, is that we need to ensure he has the tools to be happy to be left alone. We will discuss this further in part three.

To help us see life from Bob's point of view, we can use the analogy of a stress bucket. This is something you may be familiar with in human psychology. As we said earlier, we have the same basic physiology and psychology, at the emotional level, as Bob.

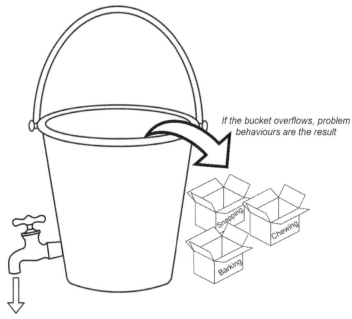

If the bucket overflows, problem behaviours are the result

Games and Activities to aliviate stress

Imagine a bucket and each time something happens, whether it is either very exciting (positive stress) or worrying (negative stress), a quantity of liquid is poured into the bucket. Over the day the bucket fills until the level reaches the threshold. When this happens, it overflows. Think about how this liquid will tip over into a box nearby. This box, when activated, results in the behaviour kept in that box. Bob reacts by barking if the barking box is triggered.

From earlier, we learned that Bob will most likely do what he did last time. The pathways (or overflows) between the stress bucket and the behaviour boxes becomes the one most used. Visualise a level where there is a hole leading down a particular shoot about halfway down the bucket. While blocking this hole may stop the behaviour box being triggered, the underlying cause of the stress bucket being filled is still there. In this case it will simply raise and find another hole and trigger a different behaviour box. Perhaps biting. This then becomes the repeated behaviour.

The behaviours in these behaviour boxes, which are triggered from being over Bobs stress threshold, are not ones we generally want. A calm dog is a happy dog, a calm Bob is a happy Bob. Behaviours chosen from the calm boxes are generally the ones we want Bob to choose. We want Bob's default to be calmness, though this applies to humans as well

To be the best we can be for Bob, we want to keep him on the happy side of the circle. If Bob has tripped over to the negative side of the wheel (the dark side, if you like) we need to make sure we can keep him calm or, at least, help him calm down. Once calm, we can work on helping him switch over to the light side (or if we're being less dramatic, the happy side).

Thankfully, there are plenty of ways to grow calmness. We need to get Bob to remain calm as his default. When this is the case, Bob will choose behaviours from the calmness boxes. When this is the case Bob will:

- Sit by your side, chill on his bed, totally relaxed may be sleeping. He will be your dream companion, the reason you wanted a dog to share your life.
- Be happier and more optimistic about life, because he will be generally lower in arousal his bucket will be a long way below threshold.

When relaxed Bob will also recover faster, his parasympathetic nervous system switches on so he can heal, digest food and conserve energy. You will be helping Bob to be happier, healthier and live a longer life.

To help with this, we will use the calmness circle below:

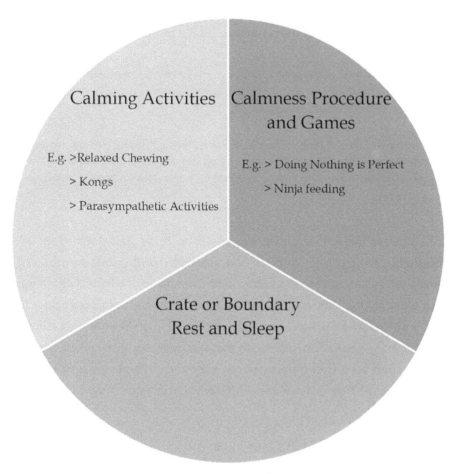

Calming Activities

First, we will begin with explaining the calming activities. In this case we want Bob to choose to engage with a Kong filled with food, maybe chew a meaty bone or simply forage for food scattered on the floor.

Chewing is an incredibly calming activity. Eating is a very relaxing activity for our companion, because of this it is also parasympathetic. This activity can help to bring Bob's arousal level down from a highly excited sympathetic, Fight or Flight, activity, to a more relaxed, parasympathetic state. Many of you will have experienced the fact that, when Bob is over excited, he will not eat. This is normal. It's the same with humans too.

> Can you think of an activity or an event that used to make you so nervous/excited? One that you could not eat beforehand? One that, as you became more practiced (and calm), that you were then able to eat before?
>
> You may find that you were able to nibble on something really tasty but could not face a full-size meal and were not interested in eating anything boring. Think about how this can be applied to Bob, who refuses to look at the kibble when excited in a distracting environment.

There are halfway activities we can use to bring Bob down from over threshold to wired then to excited, to interested and finally, to calm. The reason we include every step, is that we must take it slowly initially. We are very much taking baby steps. It will become easier and faster later on.

To understand each step, we will use this circle of emotion. An example of what a dog commonly feels is on the next page. As we improve the relationship and keep Bob calmer, we can keep the circle clear. Ultimately, we are looking for Bob to have a much clearer circle. A comparison is on the next page.

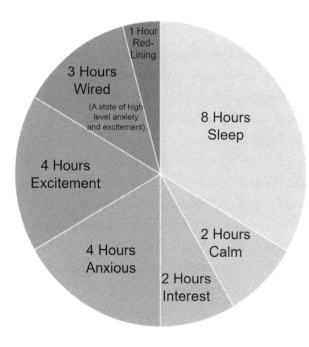

1 Hour Red-Lining

3 Hours Wired
(A state of high level anxiety and excitement)

8 Hours Sleep

4 Hours Excitement

4 Hours Anxious

2 Hours Calm

2 Hours Interest

4-6 Hours Interest & Excitement

18-20 Hours Calmness

This includes sleeping, general calmness, dozing and a relaxed interest.

Calmness Procedure

Now that we've discussed possible activities for calming Bob, we will move on to our procedure for calmness. What we're going to do is play a game called 'Doing nothing is perfect'. This is a step by step action plan to encourage Bob to choose calmness as his default position.

All you need to do is wait until Bob is calm and settled naturally. Then, simply place a medium value treat next to his head. The hope is that he will simply take the treat and stay settled. Although, it is more likely that, initially, the act of coming to him and giving him the treat will disturb him. He'll probably want to re-engage with you to garner more treats. This is where you need your most valuable skill. Self-Control. You need to ignore Bob. In this case, he will possibly engage in attention seeking behaviours. You mustn't give him the attention he seeks, instead simply go about your business.

We find one good scenario is as follows, if Bob has settled by your feet. Whether this is when you're watching tv or on your computer etc. In this case slowly place the treat (calmly with no talking) and then go back immediately to what you were doing before. The more practiced you become at treat delivery, without engaging with Bob, the better. We call this 'Ninja Feeding'.

Essentially, we are rewarding Bob doing nothing. This is powerful.

You can build this up in baby steps. To start with, as you approach with the treat, Bob may engage you. You can still give him the treat. Slowly, you build up to waiting until he is still before awarding the treat. In this instance, you are rewarding stillness.

The importance of your body language and mood state cannot be undervalued. In chapter 4.1 we will be discussing how we impact our dogs and how we may be inadvertently holding back their learning. Or, perhaps, inadvertently teaching them something we didn't intend.

With the calmness games, as you may imagine, you start playing at home. Preferably in the quietest room at the calmest time of your dog's day and when you are feeling the most relaxed. You build it up to practice at slightly busier times, then you may change the location. Try that garden before going out and about. This will likely take some time, don't worry if you're not going anywhere fast. It's much better to take your time and stay relaxed. We would say the main objective is to help Bob be calm and happy at home.

Crate or Boundary Rest

There is a simple procedure we use to help Bob choose to rest in his crate, den or bed. We're still sticking to baby steps though.

Choice is tiring. If we take choice away, it actually helps Bob to relax and sleep. Within his boundary he is away from the busy household. Nobody has any expectations of him and he has the opportunity to do what dogs do best, sleep.

> Note: As crazy as it seems, Bob actually needs 18-20 hours of sleep in a day. Often, when we're constantly trying to give Bob stimulus, we're actually exhausting him. This adds to the overall stress bucket.
>
> This is huge and instead of feeling guilty that you were out at work, you can instead know that Bob has had his much-needed rest time. However, for it to be true rest and not grief at being separated, the crate or boundary needs to be seen as a great place to be, one chosen by Bob to spend quality time.

We often see many people over stimulating Bob in the mistaken belief that they are helping to occupy and exercise him. It's surprising how life can be much easier when you realise that less is more. By making these simple changes you will find Bob is much calmer and you have more time and are feeling less pressured. When Bob has plenty of sleep, it will help prevent Bob from acting like a toddler who has not had his afternoon nap. This toddler is cranky, and nothing can please him. Once he's had that rest, and awoken refreshed, he'll be back to his normal self. Remember the parallels between animals and humans. We can be more alike that we think.

Multi-Dog households

The calmness circle works really well, especially with multi dog households. We have twelve rescue huskies, plus an additional one-to-three other Huskies who we have more recently rescued or re-homed. We work on rehabilitating these guys and finding the best forever homes for them. We also have two Jack Russells and two Retriever puppies - 10 weeks old (at the time of writing).

The only reason the household remains calm is because we have calmness as priority. Only six of the Huskies live outside full-time in our paddock (with shelters, of course). This means that there are generally quite a number of dogs in the house. Even so, it's usually quiet. All our dogs absolutely love their crates and choose to sleep, rest and relax in them.

The previous owners of the majority of huskies that come to us have already tried to use crates and often tell us that their husky will not settle in one. Not only that, but the dog actively hates them. When this is the case, it takes longer to have them actively choosing to go into the crate since they have previous negative association with them.

Fortunately, with the correct approach, it can be surprisingly easy to turn this around. Though, as always, we only take baby steps.

We seek calmness for 90-95% of the time and only have 5-10% of positive, high-excitement activity. This includes our Huskies who are known for their high energy, vocal diversity and independent minds. Calmness can be promoted by rotating between the Calmness Procedure, the Calming Activities and Rest. Given the fact that you can take turns with each dog, you can work on the calmness procedure with one or two while the others are resting or enjoying the calming activity.

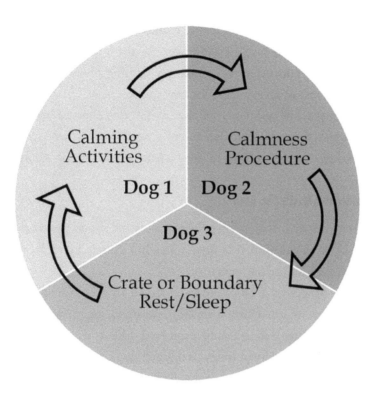

Because, in most busy households (especially those with young children or other dogs), Bob likely doesn't get the 90-95% rest that we want. His stress bucket stays full. It never really has a chance to empty. The result is that Bob is always close to the 'Red Line' or 'over threshold'.

Remember that when Bob is over threshold, he CANNOT learn. They're in such a state of stress that he has no capacity to use his brain. He's operating in the 'Fight or Flight' mode we discussed in chapter one. His higher functioning and learning part of his brain is totally bypassed in this state.

We hope this helps you to understand that Bob is not wilfully ignoring you, deliberately doing behaviour to frustrate you or simply being stubborn. It is simply, he is UNABLE to listen and learn. He will be able to if we can empty his stress bucket, keep him calm and provide positive experiences for him.

The good news is that, by playing games to teach Bob what we would like, it only takes seven or eight repetitions for them to learn rather than the four hundred repetitions if we are simply drilling obedience. Once we've achieved calmness progress becomes very quick.

The other piece of good news is that a calm dog chooses behaviours out of the calm box, these are the behaviours we would choose for our dogs to do such as resting, relaxing, walking calmly on leash or just paying attention to us.

The Yerkes-Dodson law

Now, you've noticed that we've talked quite a bit about the dog's arousal. We're going to expand on this now and while this is taken from human psychology, it applies to animals too.

To put it simply, as arousal increases up to an optimum point, performance can improve. Once over a specific threshold, performance falls. This threshold will change with training, improved skills as well as improving the ability to think and perform in arousal. Each dog or person will have their own performance curve. Train the dog in front of you.

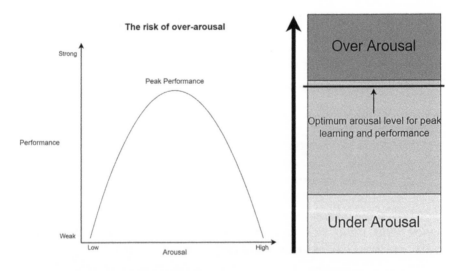

The more difficult the task, the lower arousal needs to be (aside from being asleep of course). Relatively simple, or well learned tasks, can still be accomplished when arousal is higher. We need to understand the excitement level of Bob before attempting to train anything new or a task that he finds challenging. Keep it easy, set up for success and we have easy wins.

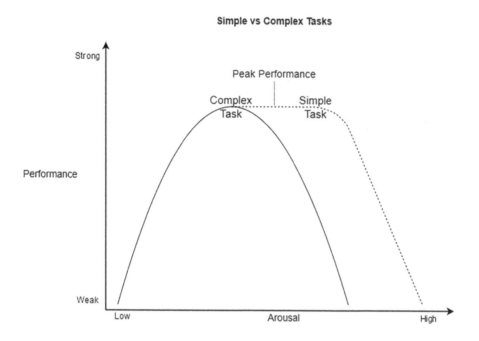

We suggest, you don't ask for anything that you're not 95% certain that Bob is able to comply with. Ask yourself this, would you bet £100 that Bob will follow your request?

The ability to think in arousal

Typical struggles which show Bob cannot think in arousal include:

- Recall being better in some locations over others; for example, at home.
- He cannot learn new behaviours unless at home, where it is quiet.
- Being so excited about the reward (e.g. a high value treat) that he cannot listen to a command. Where he's just jumping for the treat or offering a favoured behaviour when you have cued another. For example, sitting when you have asked him to lie down.
- When excited the cued trained behaviour is not as good. Where it takes a while for Bob to listen and cannot maintain any duration.

When we develop the ability to think in arousal, it means we develop a flatter curve.

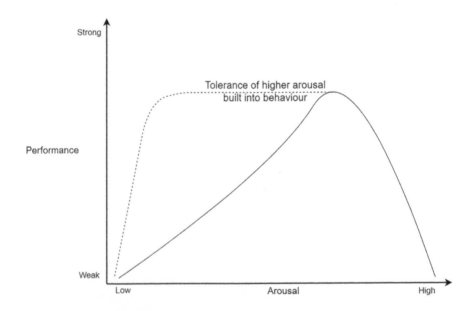

There are specific games we can play to help Bob develop this ability. All the struggles become strengths. One of these games is 'Run and Cue'. Start this game with a leash.

- While loose-leash walking at a reasonable pace, ask Bob for a behaviour he knows on cue and reward him by running ahead with him.
- As you repeat this, you will see that his arousal increases. The faster the pace, the more his arousal will increase. The more this is done, the better Bob's ability to think in arousal will improve.

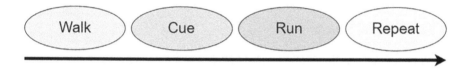

You will become Bob's expert at reading his arousal level, what type of reinforcement he needs and how it should be delivered. Remember happy and sad land.

If he's in anxiety sad land, then a lower excitement game such as calm feeding can help to switch to happy calm land. It's best to use high excitement games, reward strategies when Bob is in happy land. Below is a table with examples on how we can manipulate arousal.

Reinforcement Strategy

Arousal Level:	Low Arousal/Calm:	High Arousal/Intense:
Example reinforcement strategy choices:	Reinforcers: Kibble, Long-lasting Chews, Stroking, Access to Sniffing etc. Delivery: Calm placement to mouth, On floor, Cupping, Calm Verbal Release etc.	Reinforcers: Tug Toy, Tennis Ball, Flirt Pole, Liver Cake, Frisbee, Access to play with another dog etc. Delivery: Throwing, Catching, Chasing, Tugging, Rolling, Exciting verbal release.

A Brief Case Study

Bob was a hyper vigilant, very high energy Border Collie. His owners reported he could not settle and rest. He would constantly pace in the house. Being very vigilant he would react by barking and running towards anything that had attracted his attention. He was barking at the windows, the doorbell 'sent him crazy' in his owners' words. He would jump up at any visitor, barking and occasionally nipping them. He was unable to listen to his owners but would carry on barking and then start running around the room.

His behaviour on walks was similar. He would bark and run around the room at the sight of the leash and harness which would make it difficult to put it on him. He would sometimes nip at his owners' hands when they were putting the harness on. His barking, pulling and lunging on the leash would continue for most of the walk, escalating even further when he saw anything he was concerned about.

His owners had tried aversive, corrective techniques. An electronic barking collar was used for a while. The owners had received some complaints from neighbours about the frequency and intensity of Bobs barking. His owners reported that although this did reduce the barking, they noticed this was when the nipping started.

Bob had begun to show other behaviours which the owners believed to be showing more anxiety and even less ability to settle, causing them to stop using the collar.

Bob was living in a household with younger children, so the nipping was of much concern. He had a bed in the main living room and one in the kitchen. Mum was home most of the day with one of the younger children. She found it very difficult to take Bob on his walks with the buggy so felt guilty that he was not going out as much as she felt was needed.

To combat this, crate training was implemented. Bob had used a crate when he was a puppy. Initially to put value in the crate it was placed where Bob's bed had been, and mum kept putting food in. Kongs were put in whenever she had a few minutes. Once Bob was happy with the crate and would happily go in to chew a Kong it was placed in a quiet room at the rear of the house. A blanket placed over it.

All Bobs daily allowance of food was put into puzzle toys, Kongs etc. and fed in the crate. Classical music was played set just high enough to mask some of the external sounds that would previously have triggered the unwanted behaviour. By limiting Bobs choices (being in a crate) Bob simply lay down and went to sleep. His owners used the room as Bobs room and if Bob was sleeping then the children were not allowed to disturb him. This was the same protocol they had in place for their youngest child, so the older children found this easy to understand. They knew that if their youngest sibling did not get enough sleep he would be crying and unhappy.

Walks were discontinued for a few days, only calming games were played. Then by using calming activities in association with the harness but not going out for walks, Bob was able to have his harness on but remain calm. Short walks in quiet places were introduced. Lots of games were played in the garden at home. Bob very quickly was able to cope with longer walks and in his owners' words 'was a different dog'. The calmness protocol is continuously observed, and his owners closely monitor his stress bucket level and are happy for him to have a few days at home, playing the games in the garden when they feel it would be helpful for him.

Summary

- In this chapter we learnt about the importance of the stress bucket, the dangers of going over threshold and how that can lead to behaviours we are unlikely to want. We've introduced the calmness circles; calmness is the basis for all great choices.
- We discussed how performance (ability to learn) and arousal (excitement) interact together with how we can improve performance even in high excitement.

Mythbuster Moment: You do not need to walk your dog every day, if you need to empty the stress bucket the best thing to do is stay at home and concentrate on calmness.

We have been informed that dogs need plenty of exercise, they need two walks a day. We feel, if we have been out at work all day, we need to spend lots of time entertaining our dog. The reality is we are probably over stimulating him and not allowing enough sleep and rest time.

In the next chapter we will dig a bit deeper into how to achieve calmness, growing a bigger stress bucket with plenty of holes.

YOUR DOG'S BODY LANGUAGE

CHAPTER INTRODUCTION:

The importance of context.

Paying attention to your intuition your gut feeling
and act on it. You are your dog's advocate.

- Does a wagging tail, truly mean a happy dog? One piece of body language behaviour can mean different things in different contexts: individual behaviours have more than one meaning.
- Watching the whole dog, rather than just one area such as the trail or ears.
- Ritualised signals to help avoid and resolve conflicts.
- Canine calming signals: Averting the eyes, approaching on a curve, yawning, wagging tail etc.
- Early warning signals and taking action on the first signs. Be proactive not reactive.

A brief testimonial of a multi-dog household with two Dachshunds and a Great Dane (Fleur):

"What an eye opener! I thought I knew about dogs having owned several breeds over a period of 30 years and have learnt so much from Sonia. Realising that the same (or very similar) signal might mean different things in different circumstances has meant I now pay very close attention especially to the context. I understand my 3 dogs so much more and intervene so much earlier, being proactive rather than reactive. Fleur, Isis and Sammy are so much calmer and happier together now. I find myself watching other dogs interact and noticing signs I know I would have missed or misinterpreted before. This helps me move on and keep my dogs safe."

Dog body language is such a tricky topic, especially when not being able to demonstrate examples. We contemplated not adding this chapter but decided that we could give some tips that will help. Even with diagrams, photos, videos and real-life scenarios it is still very difficult to teach. Probably the most valuable tip is to take on board the whole picture in context.

Fleur's body language and the context it is displayed in

Like any skill, it becomes easier with practice. Often, we know how Fleur is feeling intuitively, pay attention to that feeling. Even if you are unable to describe the body language in detail to others in order to justify your decision to maybe end the encounter, avoid a situation, or even go home.

As previously discussed, dogs have many of the emotions we have and express them in their body language. We need to appreciate that different breeds and types of dog may be easier to read than others. Breed differences, motivations, and the dogs emotional state all alter the body language. Thus, context plays a primary role in correct interpretation.

For example, a dog may use a raised paw to indicate friendliness or appeasement or he may use it to be determined and demanding. It's likely that, subconsciously at least, you already know which is which with your own dog. There are several pitfalls, however, that many people fall into. There are several behavioural actions which are myths, yet many believe them:

- Fleur's tail is wagging, so she is happy and friendly.
- Fleur is rolling over, so she is submissive.
- Fleur is growling so she must be aggressive

Consider how you use labels to interpret the behaviour, it is better to state Fleur is growling rather than Fleur is showing aggression. Growling can be used as part of play. Often our huskies play rough and vocalise especially growling. Many times, this is interpreted as fighting by the owners of the other dog. Such an incorrect interpretation can lead to the husky being inaccurately labelled as aggressive.

Some signals are very subtle and easy to miss. Therefore, Fleur has to talk louder to us for us to listen – often she resorts to shouting. Consider the adage of the Englishman abroad who does not speak the language, for some reason it's incredibly tempting to simply speak louder.

We expect Fleur to be able to understand our language but often we do not make the effort to understand Fleur's language.

Canine Communication: calming signals

Dogs are social animals, and have many ways to communicate what they need, and how they are feeling. They use vocalization, and body language.

Calming signals, sometimes called displacement behaviours, help dogs to maintain great relationships and avoid negative interactions (such as fights with each other). Appeasement behaviour functions to avoid being injured in a fight. An injured animal may not survive.

These are ritualized signals, to assist in resolving conflicts.

These calming signals are used on people too. When Fleur leaves a mess on the carpet and you get upset, even though Fleur may not understand what she has done wrong, she may appear to show guilt. She is not actually feeling guilty but is using appeasement or displacement behaviours to avert the anger the human is showing. She is trying to avoid physical punishment and keep herself from being injured.

Freezing

Fleur may walk slowly or freeze when someone new approaches to show she is not threatening, or she may bow in front of a person/dog that she wants to appease. A so-called play bow is not only used to initiate play or show a desire to play, it can be used to say, 'hey I am no threat, don't hurt me'. Seemingly the same signal but check out the context – it is a completely different meaning.

Averting the eyes

Many human cultures want eye contact between each other, avoiding eye contact may be interpreted as being dishonest. Other cultures believe it to be rude and disrespectful to have eye contact under specific situations. With dogs it is considered threatening behaviour when they have direct eye contact with each other. However, a pet dog has learned to look directly at a person. If your dog wishes to look away, she is signalling one of two things, either she is nervous around you (maybe because she senses you are angry) or she is signalling a more submissive role. It makes sense with an unknown dog that you do not look directly at them, you can send a signal that you are no threat to him by looking away.

Approaching on a curve

Fleur is unlikely to approach another dog or human they don't know in a direct line, instead she will walk in a curve. This indicates that she is not aggressive and means no harm. This sends a clear signal to other dogs that all is well. If Fleur bowls straight in on a direct line and pounces on an unknown dog, it's likely not going to end well. This will depend on the other dog's personality and social skills. It is not a practice you should encourage Fleur to do. It is best if she learns a more polite way of introducing herself.

Many rehomed dogs may have missed out on key stages of socialisation and training by their mum or other family members, so they need to be taught. Meeting with people and other dogs is likely to need management whilst Fleur learns to be more respectful and polite.

Humans are often the guilty partner, by insisting Fleur meets other dogs in a direct line head-to-head and allow no appeasement gestures to take place. Usually holding the leash tightly so Fleur has no choice. Fleur cannot move away to give more space and so her anxiety escalates to fear and maybe flips over into rage. In this case, a fight may result. This is then the negative takeaway from meeting strange dogs. It is doubly sad because it has caused further anxiety in both dogs and their owners. All could have been avoided by a modified approach.

Yawning

It has become more widely known that this is one sign of stress, but again take in the context. Fleur can simply be tired. She may yawn in a social situation when she wants to tell another dog (or human) to calm down. If Fleur seems nervous or uncertain try yawning at her without looking her in the eye. Fleur may yawn too, to release her stress and calm herself down. Yawning is an automatic physical response to how Fleur is feeling. Her emotional state has triggered her adrenal system and it is now preparing gently for fight or flight. More oxygen is needed so the system takes in more oxygen by yawning.

When Fleur yawns all we really know is that her system believes she may need more oxygen. We need to understand that she may be feeling uncomfortable and we can do something about it. Other assumptions about her emotional state must come from looking at the whole picture and taking the context into account. She could be anxious, frustrated or excited.

Fleur licking her lips or nose

This is generally a self-soothing behaviour shown when she is feeling un-comfortable or uncertain in a social situation such as meeting a new dog, or person. Therefore, when feeling mild anxiety, she will lick her nose before proceeding.

Wagging tail

The myth is Fleur is happy and content when she wags her tail. Whilst this may be the case, it does depend on just how the tail is being wagged and needs to be taken in context (as always), paying attention to the rest of Fleur's body language. A nervous Fleur may wag her tail low down, or even between her back legs, it may wag very quickly.

It was mentioned earlier that different breeds of dogs will have different body language. A husky tends to greet with the tail raised high which could be interpreted as being dominant, but this is not necessarily the case. You will be the expert at knowing all the signs for when Fleur is truly happy, showing a relaxed body, no tension in the mouth, soft eyes and a happy relaxed expression.

Early warning signals: How Fleur tells us that she is uncomfortable

Do remember that when looking at Fleur it is safer to note what you see in terms of actual, observable behaviour than to make an interpretation. Train yourself to think 'tail up and rigid, shoulder muscles tense, eyes hard and staring, mouth closed' rather than Fleur is looking as if she is going to be aggressive. The context is all, it could be that she is staring at a ball when she may show the same behaviour.

The majority of the signals that Fleur gives when she feels uncomfortable are designed to benefit her in some way. It can also be that they are designed to influence another dog, or person's behaviour. Perhaps to calm the other dog, or the angry human. This will still benefit Fleur.

Intensity is very important with social species. Even simple sniffing can have another meaning if the sniffing is very intense.

Fleur may well follow a pattern of behaviour such as showing stress signs, freezing, rolling her eyes, or showing an intense hard stare. Next her head may turn away from threat with her mouth closed. She may make a low guttural growl or bark, perhaps loud and high pitch. She'll then snarl or show teeth. Then lunge snapping at the air with no contact. Finally, she'll bite. Pay attention to the first signs they may be very subtle. It is best not to let the situation escalate. Take action with the initial signs, for example the freeze or eye roll.

All behaviour seen as being a sign of stress must be read in context. Look at the whole picture. Individual behaviours do not have one single meaning. Otherwise you may think Fleur is stressed all the time.

Intense stress is bad especially when it becomes distress. A little, low level stress is fine and probably necessary. It helps us to learn, try harder, to take action etc. Stress is only bad when it reaches a level that is too uncomfortable, or when it is chronic.

Some Stress Signs				
Air Scenting	Avoiding Eye Contact	Barking	Loss of Bowel/Bladder Control	Paw Raising
Penis Crowning	Reduced Activity	Salivating	Checking Genitals	Digging
Scratching	Shaking	Shedding Hair	Dilated Pupils	Sneezing
Ears Back	Extended Tongue	Sniffing the Ground	Panting	Sweaty Paws
Lip Licking	Tail Chasing	Loss of Appetite	Over activity	Pacing
Whining	Yawning	Whale Eye	Furrowed Brow	And More...

Remember context is all. Fleur may be doing any of them for different reasons, not necessarily owing to stress. Canine communication can often be too subtle for the human to understand initially and the early warning signs can be missed. It can seem like Fleur is simply unpredictable. But, like any skill we get better with practice. As we notice the early signs and take action, we can help avoid a negative outcome.

Signs of Fear in Dogs

Slight Cowering

Major Cowering

More Subtle Signs of Fear, Stress or Anxiety

Licking Lips

when there is no food nearby

Panting

when not hot or thirsty

Brows Furrowed, Ears to Side

Acting Sleepy or Yawning

when they shouldn't be tired

Remember that you are focusing on your dog, who may express themselves differently.

A Brief Case Study

Fleur being a Great Dane was a very powerful dog and had pulled her owner over several times when on walks. She had also knocked her over in the house when following in the wake of the two excitable Dachshunds, Isis and Sammy.

We were called in to address Fleur's behaviour as this had caused several injuries (a broken arm and many bumps and bruises over multiple occasions) and her owner was unable to take her on walks and had been advised by friends and family to rehome her. The owner (Kelly) was in her 60s, devoted to all her dogs.

It soon became apparent that Fleur was reacting to the behaviour of the two Dachshunds. They were very excitable, barking, lunging and spinning both at home and especially on walks. Fleur was mirroring their behaviour. What was not seen by Kelly as a problem, was the Dachshunds. Since they were small, it didn't matter that they were jumping. Of course, this was triggering Fleurs behaviour. Kelly agreed that it would be much better if the Dachshunds were calmer, especially on walks, since she did note that the leads often became tangled around her legs. Less barking at home would please her husband although she did not mind it.

The focus was on the calmness circle, lots of chews, Kongs and setting up a quiet room. After three days remaining at home, playing calming games in the house and garden Fleur was taken on a walk without the two little guys. Kelly had practiced leash walking in the house and garden. We demonstrated figure of eight walking, circles and spirals with Fleur. Kelly was amazed by how responsive and easy Fleur was to walk on her own. Fleur is now very calm and easy to walk so Kelly feels very confident to take her out.

Kelly practiced the wombling around techniques with Isis and Sammy in her garden and then took them out on a short walk. Kelly found that they were much calmer too. It was suggested that separate walks were taken whilst work was in progress with the little guys.

Sonia pointed out to Kelly the subtle signs given by Isis which indicated anxiety, she was shown how to be proactive and manage the situation and intervene by either playing a game, such as scatter feeding or simply giving more distance. If Isis felt calm, then Sammy was also perfectly calm and quiet. The chaos was being triggered by Isis. So, Kelly is focusing on games for calmness and optimism with Isis.

Summary

- In this chapter we discussed the importance of context and watching the whole dog.
- We looked at potential warning signals that your dog may project.

Mythbuster Moment: A wagging tail means a happy dog, check out the context. Simply describe what you see rather than put a label on such as, 'a wagging tail is a friendly dog.'

Second Myth: A growling dog is an aggressive dog. Remember by checking the growling we may leave the dog with no choice but to escalate next time. This can lead to a self-fulfilling prophesy that Fleur Is aggressive.

Try spending some time simply watching as many dogs as possible and pay very close attention to the smallest signal, be proactive not reactive.

This section of the book has introduced you to the dog's end of the leash. The second section explains the importance of the environment, the context and how management is the key to helping your dog make the choices you would want.

PART 2

MANAGING THE ENVIRONMENT

MULTI-DOGHOUSEHOLDS

CHAPTER INTRODUCTION:

The importance of gated communities in multi dog and busy households.

- How to introduce a new dog into the household.
- Taking your time and using calming activities.
- The importance of creating flexibility.
- Rehearse the room. Designate rooms for calmness and rooms for excitement.
- Introducing dogs to other dogs through walking.
- The importance of vigilance and observation of all household members.
- The importance of critical socialisation periods in puppies and adolescents. Just how important is it?
- Managing uncontrolled off-leash play. You are the play police.
- Watching for bullying. This could be the newbie (even your cute puppy) bullying the older established dog.

A brief testimonial of Sheba, a female Whippet:

"I followed Sonia's advice on the steps to take when introducing my new girl, Sheba, into my household of two children (5 and 7), a Staffie boy (8) and a Lurcher girl (3). We implemented the gated community and had our guys used to that before our newbie arrived. I spent time with my children explaining why we were going to give Sheba time to settle in before they were to meet and play with her.

I arranged for them to be with my mum when Sheba first came. I noticed how, as I rotated the dogs around the rooms and boundaries, how they spent considerable time smelling the beds, rolling on and even mouthing the beds. Sonia told me to expect this as she believes they are communicating information about themselves to each other. It helps in becoming a member of the family to take on each other's scent a little and all take on a family and household common scent. Knowing to take my time and wait for what seemed intuitively the right moment, I did calm introductions with each household member. I found going on the walk perfect especially with my 2 children as it gave them something else to focus on.

One of the things I found most helpful with the coaching is how we discussed aspects of family dynamics and we sought creative solutions to things I had seen as a problem. Sonia's life experience and understanding made the solutions seem so obvious, simple and easy to do."

The Gated community

Gated communities are a very useful tool for introducing new dogs to our households. Whether these are "puppy" pens, gates, doors, crates or simply beds, we often need to keep the dogs separated initially.

How do we introduce new dogs to our household to get the best possible start?

To start with, there will be no direct meeting. It is better that the dogs see each other with more distance and keep well within their individual comfort zones. They can become familiar with each other's smell by rotating between rooms, crates and boundaries. Many people try to rush this. You are likely to be excited and a bit nervous when bringing your new guy home. Take a moment to think about this and set Sheba and the others, together with any other family members, up for success. First impressions last. It is better not to start with a repair job.

Remember, when a dog first arrives (particularly if being rehomed) they are likely to be very stressed. We refer back to our stress bucket. At the point of arrival, they're likely close to overflowing. This means they are highly likely to choose behaviours that are not wanted. They are likely to be experiencing negative emotions, at a high level of intensity, which rarely ends well.

It is best to opt for following all aspects of the calmness procedure for several days, as discussed in 1.3. It can take a week for the stress cortisol levels to drop sufficiently. Your other family members are likely to also have more stress in their buckets than usual on account of the new arrival.

Avoiding excitement is best even though you may wish to play high energy fun games. One of the best activities to do is scent work. Don't worry if you don't know if your new dog has done any formal scent work before, the beginner stages are very straight forward. This is discussed in more detail in chapter 3.4.

When Sheba is smelling the environment, she is using up to 41% of her brain. This is a very pleasant task for her, not only that, but it is also very calming. When she has finished, she will be pleasantly tired, it's an activity that uses plenty of thought. She is likely to be ready to have a snooze. This is perfect for what we want.

Don't be in a hurry for meeting the other family dogs. It is a good thing for the newbie to bond with you for a few days. You need to be the important one to them, not the other household dogs. If you can pay into your new relationship bank account right from the start, then you are on the quickest path to success.

What we don't want, are head-to-head meetings with the others until we know that all household members will make the right decisions. For multi dog households (or those with children in various combinations) stair gates give a degree of separation. Many people say, "My house is too small for crates". The truth is that small houses can be so much more tranquil. When this is the case, suddenly it feels like there is more room.

When several dogs are running around, doing zoomies, barking and/or lunging it can feel as if the house is too small. Having these gated communities makes it feel like there is more room. It keeps the environment tranquil, calm and pleasant for the household. You are essentially rehearsing the rooms for calm and quiet.

It is a good Idea to have crates underneath tables. Especially if space is limited. We usually have crates underneath our desks. This means that we can crate train new guys whilst we work. During the time of this writing, there two new rescue Huskies relaxing in a crate each whilst two Jack Russells and two other Huskies are free, having not been cued to a boundary or crate. Though, funnily enough, they have chosen to find a crate to snooze in anyway. They are a mixture of boys and girls and we have a peaceful environment. This is precisely what we want.

When we're teaching our dogs their boundaries, we want to create a level of flexibility in them. The hope is that each dog will voluntarily go onto any of the boundaries we have. When we have this, we can rotate dogs to different rooms to give them a change of scene, knowing that they will settle happily. No matter where you want them to be.

We choose to play games in specific rooms. This give certain rooms the associations of being places where calmness is expected. Going into one of the calm rooms and requesting to go in a crate means, 'let's just go to sleep'. We generally place covers over the crates to turn them into more of a den. There is then less visual stimulation to make it easier for Sheba to choose to remain calm. We can, and do, raise and lower the covers depending on what we want her experience to be and if we feel that Sheba will remain calm.

In our case, all the dogs can see each other and can interact but have chosen to just relax. The choice we want. We will rotate them around later, bringing the new huskies out of the crates and the established group into them. We're not yet ready for our new dogs too meet the others. It's all about taking baby steps. We won't move forward with the next stage unless we believe there is a 95% chance of success.

In Sheba's case, with another two dogs in the house, she can be given a Kong so she rehearses the room as being calm and not a place for zoomies and barking. We need to communicate to the other household dogs that Sheba is a non-event and of no concern. We can give the other dogs Kongs or other calming activities (as we discussed in chapter 1.3), so they feel Sheba is something positive. There should be no direct interaction until we are positive it will go well.

Often, dogs don't know what is good for them, or the best way to introduce themselves. They may be lacking is doggie social skills, so we need to be vigilant, keep things calm and positive.

Introducing our dogs

It's preferred when we are introducing our dogs that we walk in a quiet area with as few distractions as possible. It is best with one person per dog. The person has Sheba on her left, and the other person has the other dog on her right. Thus, to start with, the people are in between the dogs. A good idea would be to start on opposite sides of the road or path. If you're in the open, then keep a rough twenty-foot distance between the dogs.

As the walk progresses all we need to do, is casually closing the gap. The dogs will be on a short leash in a heel position. We also don't want overtly to be paying too much attention to the dogs. We want to seem like we're simply focussing on moving forward, calmly and it is not a big deal. It's even better if the people simply have a chat. We're role modelling calmness. As you progress with your observation skills you will notice very small changes in tension or anxiety levels and proactively move apart to give more distance to avoid a potential negative event. Thus, even though you seem not to be focusing on Sheba intensely and potentially putting pressure on her you are still in tune with her and ready to act appropriately.

If tension does accrue, then simply increase the distance and keep walking. It is important to plan together beforehand so each person knows their role before starting and what to do if things don't go as well as hoped. The main thing is to be calm yourself, we talk more about this in part four.

Before we start, it's a good plan to have walked Sheba separately in the area you are planning to walk the dogs together. This means that she has already seen the area and knows what to expect. Choose an area that she was comfortable with.

Once the dogs are walking calmly side by side, you may feel the time is right for some off-leash interaction. We choose a fenced field or garden where there is plenty of space. After walking around it a few times casually take both leads off but keep walking forward. Stay chatting so that there is no pressure on the dogs. We will only progress to this point after all the signs so far have been good. Where they've been in the house for a few days and been comfortable with each other on the walk.

The choice of the first dog we're introducing to Sheba is important. You will know which is your easy going, well socialised guy and choose him or her. We generally find that if we have a new boy we introduce with a girl and vice versa. The personality of the dog is more important than gender. Dogs do have likes and dislikes of other dogs and can surprise us on their choices.

When we're introducing the dog to the household, we must be a little more methodical. We want to keep them separated, initially in different rooms. We need to watch their general body language and keep an eye on their stress bucket. Keep practicing calming activities, not just with Sheba, but with all the dogs.

Before we remove the barriers separating our dogs, we must 'rehearse the room' beforehand. We want the house to be totally calm, that includes the people and the dogs. We're taking baby steps constantly and keeping everything casual. Only making the first introductions when it genuinely feels right. If you have any doubts, then keep practicing and delay the introductions. It is much easier for the future when first impressions are favourable. The best thing to hope for is when they don't much bother with each other and do nothing. We can add the fun, games and excitement when we know it is safe to do so.

Depending on the newbie's personality and behaviour we may sometimes use other approaches. We may utilise the role modelling from happy, confident dogs. If we have a very sensitive, timid newbie who is wary of humans (therefore us) then if they are happy with other dogs, they can join in with the group and watch their new friends interact with us. This can also be done from the safety of their crate or gated area. They can watch but feel safe with no pressure placed on them. If a newbie is worried about people, then one person is best to avoid overwhelming them.

When we feel that the time is right and that the household is calm, we can think about removing the barriers. It's important that we're role modelling calmness, we must project that what we are doing is 'no big deal'. We want Sheba to be on a long, loose leash. We want the boundary games to be fresh in her head, so play some beforehand. We discuss boundary games later in the book. Once she is resting on her bed or boundary, we will remove the gate which is separating her from the rest of the household. We're giving Sheba the option to meet the others, but we want to reward her choice to stay on the boundary.

It's vital that the gate is only removed when the other dogs are in a similar 'chill' state. We want them to be resting in the same, or an adjoining room, but ignoring Sheba. This, of course, relies on our other dogs to be used to remaining relaxed when you are playing games with another dog. This must be practiced so that they remain calm in preparation for this moment.

Vigilance and observation of our own dogs is paramount throughout. The household stress bucket needs to be empty. This certainly includes children. We suggest that the dogs meet each other in the absence of children initially. Remember, we always want to take baby steps and continuously practice calming activities, keeping our own emotions calm and being confident. If we are concerned, or anxious, then it is best for someone who is genuinely calm to make the first introductions. When we have seen all is well, we may feel more confident and trusting that all will be fine.

Set up for success from day one.

Now we have discussed introductions for adults and other dogs we're going to talk about children. Hopefully, you can introduce any older children in the same way as other adults, often best on a walk or when simply chatting and relaxing at home. This allows Sheba to make any first contact, maybe keep a leash on for extra safety.

If you have younger children in the household then you probably have checked your newbie's reputation for being good with children. But, re-member the stress bucket. It is likely when the new dog arrives her bucket will be full so she may not choose the behaviour you wish. Do not be in a hurry to introduce them to each other.

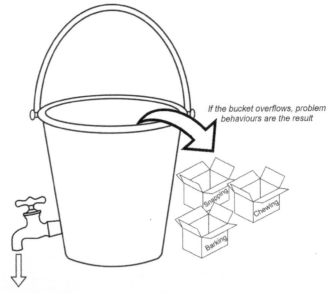

If the bucket overflows, problem behaviours are the result

Snapping *Chewing* *Barking*

Games and Activities to aliviate stress

Calmness is equally important for the children, maybe best meet the new dog after they have had their playtime and are relaxed themselves. We always supervise young children and animals and not just on first meetings. If we are not present, we pop the dog away. Children need to know the rules too. If Sheba is in her crate, or on her boundary, then everybody should leave her to sleep.

Households with young children are often not calm households. It is very important that the dogs all have a place to move away from the bustle. This would be the same if a person has special needs, or maybe acts in a way that may add to the stress bucket (for example, sudden shouting). This is where crates are awesome. They can be in a quiet room and you can have peace of mind knowing that the dogs are safe, resting, and emptying their buckets. You can see the value of taking the time to put the value in the crates/boundaries. Remember how much sleep a dog needs.

When we rehome a dog, we want to provide the best possible forever home. What may have been the best practice and advice in the past, may not be the best advice for now and the future. Education moves on, when we know better, we do better. This applies to all aspects of life.

In the 80s the advice centred on the idea of dominance and having alpha roles with the idea that the human was supposed to be alpha. This theory has been discredited and certainly does not apply to domestic dogs. It was based on the behaviour of wolves but, was actually flawed research and does not even apply to the ordinary wolf family. We talk about this more in chapter 4.2.

It would be natural to consider that the newly acquired rescue dog, Sheba, may need the same kind of training that a puppy may need with regard to socialisation. We may set off with enthusiasm and determination to follow the principles we learnt with our earlier dogs. Again, much of the original puppy socialisation has also been shown to be counter-productive in many cases.

The aim was to give a form of stress immunisation by introducing them to as many people, dogs etc as possible. In many cases the puppy becomes more fearful having been over stimulated and over excited. This can happen to your newbie. Less is more. Take your time. Friends and family may encourage you to just let them get on with it, this may or may not work depending on the personalities of the dogs and the context. If it goes pearshaped then a repair process takes much longer, and trust is sacrificed. We have not kept our dogs safe.

Rescue and rehoming

Many people are aware of critical socialisation periods in dogs. Critical socialisation periods as a puppy, then adolescent and teenage sensitive periods. Sadly, many dogs are put into rescue in their adolescent period when the cuteness and novelty factor has worn off, together with the fact that the dog is now so much bigger and stronger. It is particularly sad that many dogs have the emotional trauma of being put in rescue at this time. All is not lost however, when we can understand Sheba's struggles, we are better placed to help with compassion and patience.

Ensure that the new rescue, whether young or old is respectful with other and older dogs at home. Be your dog's expert and advocate, you are responsible for all the dogs being happy. Not just the newbie.

It is easy to fall into the trap of allowing the new guy to play too roughly and too much with your exciting dog or dogs. Possibly because you feel sorry for her and want to make up for her past sad life. It is easy to feel pleased at how happy the new dog seems because she is confidently playing and enthusiastic. You may equally be very happy about how tolerant your other household dogs are of Sheba. You may have chosen a particularly calm guy for your first introduction. But if you have not read the signs correctly and do not intervene when necessary it can easily lead to the new dog bullying your other dogs.

This is very stressful for your original dogs, plus it is counter-productive to how you would like the new rescue to behave when meeting other dogs on walks. Sheba is likely to use the same approach, which will again intimidate other dogs, or leash to fights, angry owners and possibly vet bills. As you then have to keep your new rescue away from other dogs to avoid such incidents, she is likely to feel very frustrated and choose the behaviours out of the over-excited box.

The above can all be avoided by careful baby steps, promoting calmness and a proper introduction where the aim is not full on play but rather a calm, polite greeting. Something similar to having a quick sniff and moving on to interact again with you. You want to be more important than the environment, that includes other dogs. Remember how you spent the first few days bonding with your newbie before she met the rest of the family?

Rules of engagement

Our rules of engagement are to think in terms of teamwork and partnership not hierarchy and dominance. Socialisation is not 'my dog has to play with every dog'. Socialisation is about learning to socially interact with other living things. This may be people, dogs, cats, horses or any living thing that the dog needs to come into regular contact with, especially within the household.

Always keep the end in mind. See the dog that is yet to be, see their potential. Yes, we need to be forgiving and kind, but it's best to always start off as we mean to go on. For example, if we do not want our dog to jump up on people then we need to prevent this at the beginning. It is very easy with a young rescue to allow them to perform behaviours that you later need to change. If they have practiced such behaviours regularly then they are hard to address. Early experience carefully managed can help towards final picture. Wrongly done, it may cause or exacerbate what was on the cards. Think about how we want the behaviour to be, don't let young dogs practice any behaviour that we don't want as an adult. Do not assume they will grow out of such behaviour. What they have been rewarded for, and enjoyed, they will repeat.

Avoid socialisation experiences that mean your rescue is being handled by lots of other people. Direct observation shows that most people are novice handlers and are likely to be thinking of their own dogs or other things rather than concentrating on the rescue they are handling. They will probably not be able to read canine body language and will make mistakes. This can sensitise the new guy to being handled and even the environment in which it is being done.

Instead, ensure that first experiences are done in a manner that you are in control of. Constantly calm without too many people while being clear with how you would like your guy to be handled. Set clear boundaries for what you feel is appropriate.

A Little bit of stress may be ok. It may even be seen as exciting. Stress that is too much results in mental, emotional and physiological changes. Chronic damaging stress not excitement. Play it safe and always think about calmness. Keep checking body language and be ready to intervene. If you do then take control quietly and with confidence, stop the session if necessary. Think about subsequent bucket emptying activities.

When we think about the stress signs, think of the four F's. Fight, Flight, Freeze and Flirt (or Fiddle about). The fight and flight responses are fairly well known. The early warning signs can be easy to miss though. The Freeze response is often overlooked and then is often followed by one of the other responses. Flirting is used as coping strategy, this can be showing random 'giddy' type of behaviour or flopping on the floor totally limp like a sack of potatoes.

There is perhaps a fifth F for Flock, taken from human psychology. When people become fearful outside, they cluster together for social reassurance. Clearly many animal species do this; very obviously with prey animals. Dogs do this too. They may use people to flock to for reassurance. If

Sheba runs to us outside, goes behind us or jumps up for reassurance then make sure we don't ignore what may be a cry for help.

If Sheba is showing any of the five F's she is feeling negative emotions and you need to intervene quickly. Think about going home, emptying the bucket and maybe staying home for several days to ensure the cortisol has been removed from the body. Best of all, avoid any situations where you are not 95% certain Sheba will be happy. Remember to control the environment.

Knowing your dog's body language helps to assess dogs rapidly, reduce stress and marries your head and your gut instinct. If you listen to your intuition you will know how your dog is feeling. If you learn to objectively read the signs as well, you will be able to describe them to others. They will then understand more fully and realise that you are not being over-protective or fussy. Even if they think you are, carry on and protect your dog's wellbeing. You are her advocate. You need to keep yourself, your dog and others safe.

Experienced and confident handlers

Handling needs to be associated with positives and based on choice. Always allow Sheba to move away. Only carry on if given the green light. A good test of if the handling is acceptable, is if you move away then Sheba follows and re-initiates the handling.

This approach is demonstrated successfully with wild animals. It is far better that Sheba feels she has a choice and some control. Especially with rescue dogs that in the past have been handled with dominance and given no choice. Do not carry on doing something until Sheba has stopped struggling. This is very stressful and seriously undermines the trust relationship. It could have led to fight responses in the past and may trigger similar behaviour.

Uncontrolled off leash play

Remember your end picture, you probably do not want Sheba to get over excited when she sees other dogs and expect to go off and play. Especially if it means you lose her ability to recall. Before letting Sheba go off to play with other dogs it is best to have individually assessed the other dogs and check that they can be recalled, have good dog socialisation skills and you are comfortable that their owner is aware of Sheba's needs. It is best to start with one new, previously assessed, dog at a time and keeping any play sessions short. Three- minute play sessions as a maximum. Mix dogs according to confidence levels. Remember the bucket filling.

It is better when Sheba learns to say hello politely and then moves on with you rather than be obsessed playing with the other dogs. If we visit the vet, we want our dog(s) to ignore and be calm with other animals, not anticipate a mad play session.

If you decide to join in with a class activity, then check the trainer knows the other dogs' personalities and your dog's needs. It is best if you have had a one to one session with them beforehand, so you have confidence in them.

Prevent barrier frustration

An example may be when dogs are on the leash and pulling to reach each other. This can be difficult to prevent in group sessions, especially if there is not much room. You may have noticed that Sheba is much better playing off the leash and is 'reactive' on the leash. Intervene before this happens. Avoid the situation so she does not practice the behaviour you don't wish her to choose. Be proactive, change direction and give more room and maybe scatter feed if appropriate. When scatter feeding, simply spread part of their daily ration in the garden where Sheba can forage for it.

Bullying

Finally, watch out for Sheba practicing bullying at home. The older dog is typically very tolerant and lets the newbie beat up on them. This may also happen with cats being intimidated. Sheba may bully people too. She may want to have everything her own way: 'I want to go for walk, have a biscuit, have attention'. What gets rewarded gets repeated. This is not a dominance issue, just a learning experience.

Dog to dog aggression: Younger dogs who bullied in the home, statistically, were worse with other dogs outside as they had been used to bullying their older dog companion. This often led to a dog-to-dog aggression problem with other dogs later. It may be that your dogs need separate walks, training, habituation etc.

A Brief Case Study

Alison, the parent of two dogs and two children, contacted me for advice on the best way to introduce a new dog Sheba to their busy household. We had previously helped Alison with her Lurcher girl Belle. Alison, therefore, already had a working knowledge of the importance of calmness, together with playing games for recall and loose leash walking. Alison had met her new whippet Sheba and described her as nervous, timid and with limited dog socialisation experiences. She had, of course, fallen in love with her and was determined to help her.

We had a consultation via skype so I could outline the techniques for introducing a new dog to a household. Then a bespoke plan was drawn up as to how Alison could best proceed. The importance of first impressions was discussed together with emphasising utilising all the calmness protocols. Allowing Sheba to bond with Alison in a safe, calm and happy setting for a few days was strongly advised. Suggestions were made as to how Alison could explain to her children, family and friends as to why they were not going to meet Sheba immediately. Given Sheba's personality this was particularly important.

Alison arranged for her children to be elsewhere and the house to be quiet. Her husband had taken Belle and Billy out on a long walk. He had used the car so when he arrived home, he could

leave them in the car to check all was well before he brought them in. This gave Alison time to ensure she was in another room with Sheba when they entered the house. Alison had spent the time introducing Sheba to the rooms she intended to use initially.

For a few days with Sheba, Alison and her husband Brian provided a calm, reassuring presence and kept the household as quiet as possible. This was important as Sheba's stress bucket was full thus giving the time for it to empty and for her to feel as safe, calm and happy as possible.

Gradually Alison introduced Sheba to other rooms in the house, she rotated the rooms where the other dogs were kept so they could learn each other's scents, see each other in safety with plenty of distance.

Alison and Brian decided to introduce the dogs on a walk. Both Billy and Belle now had great loose leash walking skills. This went well so they decided to allow a full introduction. They did this with their calmest dog Billy first. The session was kept very short, then they were returned to more calmness protocols and sleep. The following day, another short walk and the introduction to Belle. Again, a short introduction which went well. This was in an enclosed area so they could be off leash in safety. Belles recall was excellent so they had the confidence to know they could intervene if necessary. Sheba was on a long line.

Events proceeded very quickly after this, increasing the exposure time, keeping a careful eye on monitoring body language and supervising. Other family members were introduced after care was taken to explain beforehand about Sheba being worried and likely to be frightened by loud noises and quick movements. Again, sessions were initially kept short with proactive intervention when believed necessary.

After the three days of calmness protocol at home, games for optimism, proximity and novelty were introduced. Games where there was no expectation or pressure were used first. Alison was very careful to ensure that Sheba remained relaxed, taking baby steps and following the 95% rule.

Sheba is now fully integrated to her new household, she has a much more optimistic personality, clearly showing joy in playing the games. She loves playing with the children having become used to their noise and high energy. Alison is currently working on recall (perfect at home, in the garden but not 100% in high distraction areas. Alison is careful to protect her from meetings with other dogs (or humans) that she believes would be inappropriate for her. This guards Sheba's optimism.

Summary

- Dogs are learning 24/7, not just when we think we are training. First impressions do last so ensure you have a plan for introductions. We follow the theme from previous chapters where there is an emphasis on calmness. Calmness is the key to a happy dog. Remember to rehearse the room for calmness and always take baby step, only do something if you are 95% sure that it will end in success.

- Take your time introducing a newbie, pay attention to everybody's body language. There is a group stress bucket too. Start off as you mean to go on, look to the goal and work backwards from there. For example, if you do not wish your newbie to jump up as an end goal, consider how you can avoid her practicing this behaviour from the first day.

- Management is training. By controlling the environment, you are preventing rehearsal of behaviour you do not want and are setting up for success for the choice of behaviour you do want.

Mythbuster Moment: 'I should be able to train my dog to do what I want, when I want by giving rewards and by ignoring the behaviour I do not want.' This will not work in many real-life situations. Sometimes ignoring the behaviour is not possible or safe, it may be self-rewarding behaviour, so even if you are ignoring it the activity itself is the reward and so the behaviour will be repeated.

In the next chapter we will introduce how ditching the routine and ditching the feed bowl can help in management of stress levels and help to build calmness.

2.2

DITCH THE BOWL AND ROUTINE

CHAPTER INTRODUCTION:

Looking at practical ways that ditching the bowl and the routine can help with car journeys and general life.

- Ditch the bowl, ditch the routine.
- Seeking and working for food, an enrichment activity.
- Interacting with your dog, enjoy the social and playful side of seeing their food.
- Add value to crates and boundaries through food.
- Food puzzles and scent games for a mental work-out and a release for stress.
- Introduction to travel, ensuring your dog is stress free when travelling.
- Effective use of holistic therapies to ease travel sickness and stress.

A brief testimonial of Sox, a female Springer Spaniel:

"The single thing of ditching the bowl transformed our life with Sox. She was a dog who wasn't food motivated or interested and so I found it difficult to train her using rewards. Now, she's turned into a different dog. She loves working and playing the games. She was always a bit skinny and has put on some weight, which I am happy about. Ditching the routine has helped to stop her from being overexcited at our usual walk time, and I realise now that she was over threshold before we even left the house. I can play the games, scatter feed and keep her calm and attentive to me on the whole walk.

The advice about travelling was so helpful. From being with a dog who was howling and drooling the whole car journey we now have peace and quiet. Even better, I know Sox is no longer stressed by travelling.

I loved learning about why she was behaving as she was. She joined my family three years ago when she was two. She had made some progress becoming less fearful and lets me stroke her, even though she may still be anxious. The information about the stress bucket and going over threshold sparking off behaviour patterns like her spinning and barking was fascinating. I have followed the advice and I am so happy with the transformation. She is now a loving, calm, happy little girl. She even chooses to meet some people with who she feels comfortable. She is great with all family and friends now, no longer trembling and trying to hide."

Dogs need routine, right? So why are we saying ditch the routine?

This may seem a daunting task at first. One that seems at odds with everything we have often been told about owning a dog. It has become the norm to give proprietary dog food – wet, tinned or dry kibble. This food is generally marketed as being a balanced diet with all the correct vitamins, minerals etc. We have been taught to feed once or twice a day (more if a puppy) with all the information given on the packaging as to quantity for the specific breed, age and weight. Dogs have their own feed bowls, often a set time and routine for feeding. Routine has often been stated as being extremely important.

So, as the heading states, ditch the bowl. What do we mean by that? Well, Sox is not going to be fed from her bowl anymore and, to add to the novelty, she will no longer have a set routine.

Ditch the bowl, ditch the routine.

It is, generally speaking, the human member of the partnership who is attached to the routine. We do fully understand, given the constraints of work, we often find it easier to follow a specific routine, especially in the morning, before leaving for work. We can discuss some easy, quick, creative solutions.

Why ditch the bowl and why ditch the routine?

In chapter 1.2 we discussed the importance of seeking behaviour and how it is a primary drive. We mentioned that dogs are programmed to sniff, hunt and search for their food. The anticipation of the finding of the food is more rewarding than the actual eating. If we are to simply give Sox her food in a bowl, we are doing her a disservice. We are taking away a great opportunity to fulfil a major drive. All the value of the food is simply in the bowl, so often Sox has a great relationship with her bowl. Wouldn't it be better if she had the great relationship with us instead? By ditching the bowl, we are enriching Sox' life.

If we are not going to use the dog bowl how will we give Sox her food?

You can be very creative and do as much or as little as fits into your busy schedule. Mix it up to suit you. You can still do this with multi-dog households, in fact it is a bonus if you do. This goes hand in hand with ditching one aspect of routine: mealtime.

Remember, dogs love to interact with you and enjoy the social, playful side of seeking their food. Set puzzles, tasks and learning games for mealtime. The more you use food to interact with Sox the more addictive and enjoyable it becomes for both of you.

Weigh out Sox's daily ration of food. For some non-foody dogs, we suggest weighing out their weekly ration. Some dogs have a day or two where they choose not to eat. Huskies are especially notorious for this. Many people worry that their dog is very picky about eating and believe they will not want to 'work' for their food. In fact, the opposite is generally the case. A fussy Sox may suddenly become very food motivated and will follow various cues with enthusiasm to earn a piece of kibble that she had previously turned her nose up at and left it in the bowl.

> Do remember, manufacturers are going to err on the side of giving too much food rather than too little with their guidelines. Be guided by the good condition of Sox.

It used to be the norm to give dogs a day off from eating. It was viewed as having health benefits. This, together with mimicking the fact that dogs as scavengers, would have originally gone a day or two as a matter of course without being successful at finding food. Now it is common for people to worry if their dog has not eaten for a day.

By interacting and playing games, using food is an amazing way to bond and bring joy to the relationship. Sox will find it hugely rewarding to work for her meals. It gives the relationship bank account huge pay ins and it means Sox is less likely to seek her own creative ways of occupying herself.

By ditching the bowl and feeding the daily ration in other ways, we can help give value to boundaries and crates. You can choose to put various food-based puzzles, Kongs, bones etc in the crate. When doing this, you are ticking two boxes: entertaining Sox and giving

value to the crate/bed/boundary. Take advantage of this easy way to achieve the behaviours you do want.

We suggest closing the crate door (when Sox is ready for that stage) or securing the puzzle toy/food filled Kong or bone to the place you wish Sox to have value for. Otherwise, she will simply take it to where she prefers. This option is fine if you are happy with her choice.

Interactive puzzle toys are great for stimulating Sox and giving her a mental work-out. When Sox uses her brain, she is ready to have a rest afterwards. Just like us, if we have been really concentrating then we feel both mentally and physically tired. This means we have kept the bucket empty, using the brain. Licking, chewing and eating help with calming. (remember the science behind this). You can be inventive and make your own interactive food puzzle toys. There are plenty that can be purchased such as slow feeder bowls and puzzle toys.

Food can also be hidden in Snuffle mats or wrapped in cloth/towels etc as a low arousal activity and a great way to engage Sox' brain.

When time is short, then scatter feeding is the answer. Simply scatter part of the daily ration ideal in the garden where Sox can sniff it out from the grass. You can also choose to scatter feed in the house, you decide if the kitchen is best for this.

> Note: With all the above ways of dispensing the daily ration, make it very easy at first for Sox to be successful. Maybe raising the value of the food to be discovered. If it is too difficult, Sox may find it too frustrating with the corresponding negative emotion.

Start the transition of ditching the food bowl by getting Sox to chase the food in your hand, target it and then bowl a piece of food away for them to chase. Later, you can restrain the food slightly (if safe to do so) and then throw it. If you know they will go after it then give a cue like 'get it'.

Another method is by using a Kong. Pack a large one with food that will just fall out when it is pushed around. To add challenge later on you can pack it a little tighter, perhaps use a paste to bind the contents. Finally, try freezing it. Start slowly in this case and work up to freezing it overnight. This is especially rewarding on hotter days and is a great activity for bringing arousal levels down. It almost becomes automatic that Kong equals settle down.

There are many types of long-lasting chews that can be given, be aware of choosing a healthy alternative.

It is always the same procedure with any new game or challenge. Keep it very easy at the start, set up for success and first start in a 'boring' setting. One with few other distractions. You can try in other more distracting settings as you go. For example, scatter feeding can be done when out on a walk. It will help to keep calmness as eating is a parasympathetic activity. Gradually building up the ability for Sox to be able to take food on walks will be a great step forward. Many dogs are unable to do so as their sympathetic system is so switched on and their buckets are too full.

Remember baby steps and the 95% rule.

The daily rations can be given in stuffed toys, puzzle toys, snuffle mats and by scatter feeding. No matter your dog's diet, food can be delivered in this manner. Yes, even if you raw feed. Try chopping it up, freezing it or even purchasing freeze dried alternatives. It can be given in a treat dispenser, as squeeze tube, rolled into meatball (use a mould and freeze, even use a spoon if you don't wish to handle the food). This can all be prepped the day before, using the fridge and freezer or cool boxes. Usually mornings before work are not the ideal time to start filling Kongs.

The rest of the ration can be given by playing awesome games especially ones that involve feeding from our hand. This really skyrockets our relationship bank account. There are literally hundreds of games you can play. The only limit is your creativity. We will suggest several to get you started in a later chapter but, it is even more fun to make up your own.

As will be discussed later, there are specific games that help with specific concepts such as confidence, optimism, dealing with frustration, arousal up, arousal down, focus and proximity. These games will rocket your progress towards your goals of loose leash walking, recall, being able to ignore distractions and keeping their focus on you.

> The magic happens by a combination of preventing the rehearsal of what you don't want (managing the environment), promoting calmness, keeping their stress bucket emptied (growing a bigger bucket with a bigger hole for emptying) plus playing fun games to teach concepts.

This results in the dog of your dreams. One that is happy, confident, calm and who actively wants to follow your direction. A dog that is secure and has a fully enriched life.

Introduction to travel. How ditching the routine can be applied to travel.

When we see a piece of behaviour as painful and difficult for Sox, we have more compassion, and we behave accordingly, with patience. When we view it as problem behaviour, the dog being naughty/bonkers we are more likely to view it negatively. We're likely to react with emotions of frustration and behave in a negative, unhelpful way. This applies across the board with any animal species and within our relationship with others.

One common struggle is when Sox does not settle in the car, she may drool excessively, bark incessantly, whine, pace (if not secured), and/or vomit. She may lick her lips, yawn and pant, whine and pant, she may urinate or defecate (if very anxious). One in six dogs suffer from travel sickness.

Motion sickness can be caused by a number of factors, though, primarily it is caused by movement in the inner ear. This is most commonly seen in puppies and young dogs, as the ear structures used for balance are not fully developed, so they may outgrow it. However, some don't. There is a mismatch of stimuli when visual input does not correspond with movement and spatial orientation.

If Sox connects the negative travel sickness with the car, she may develop signs of stress even before getting in the car. This can add to the sickness. Classic signs are inactivity, listlessness, uneasiness and excessive drooling.

To make the rides as comfortable as possible we can do a list of things which include:

- Ensuring she faces forward rather than looking out the side window.
- Opening the windows to balance the air pressure.
- Making sure the car is cool and well ventilated.
- Limiting the food intake before a journey.

These may sound familiar if you suffer from motion sickness yourself. You can also purchase an anti-static leash; we have had good results from using newspaper on the floor. It is believed that it absorbs the static electricity.

Try lavender oil for calmness and drive carefully, avoiding unnecessary braking and acceleration.

Several of our rescue dogs initially had some struggles with travel, but the same principles that you have been introduced to in earlier chapters apply. We always take baby steps, focus on calmness and control the environment so the behaviour cannot be expressed. This, together with ditching the routine, cuts out the excitement generated by expectation and anticipation.

It is very likely that when Sox sees all the preparation for travel, she is already becoming anxious and excited. Remember when excitement is added to the mix of anxiety it can lead to fear, or even the rage response.

We want to get rid of the anticipation that the car means an exciting activity, or the negative emotion previously felt. Find our where Sox's calm, comfortable zone is around the car. In the absence of any triggers, such as you preparing for a journey or touching leashes etc., it is ideal if you can do this with the car parked in your drive or a secure, fenced area so Sox can be off-leash. It is all about her choice and her feeling in control rather than trapped, coerced, or under any pressure. Less stress is felt when we feel we have choice and control.

Initially, you can scatter feed in the comfort zone (where no signs of anxiety are exhibited), gradually getting closer. Be very calm and casual yourself, treat it just the same as scatter feeding in other areas in your house or garden. If you feel Sox is ready (you are the expert with the stress signs and your dog) you can toss some food into the car. Leaving doors open. Remember, it's her choice. You can then put some chews or filled Kongs in the car. It's a similar process to crate training; you want Sox to associate the car and its crate with calmness, a positive, happy emotion. Like crate/boundary training, you can close the door when you feel the time is right, when you are 95% certain she will remain calm and keep chewing. Extend the periods remembering to vary the duration so you are not always making it harder. Throw in lots of easy wins.

Once you feel she is ready, you can start the engine but remain stationary. It is a good idea to do an activity yourself that Sox associates with nothing is happening now, for example, answering some emails. Move on to a very short journey but don't get out the car, simply return home. Give her another chew or Kong, chill and then open door. Allow the choice of remaining with food in the car. Extend the time of the journey when first leaving the car and having a walk, keep it low in excitement, play some calming focus games and return home. You are building up calm and positive associations in place of the previous negative emotions of anxiety plus excitement which may have led to fear or rage.

When you do need to go for a journey do your preparation in as calm a manner as possible. Even better is if Sox goes out for a calming walk and plays calming games out of sight. Then, with the absence of triggers, just head off in the same way as previous shorter journeys. This is where you need to be aware of your own excitement over the journey. Sox will pick up on this and mirror it back to you.

Be aware of any legal requirements for travelling as regard to the country where you live. In the UK dogs must be secured so they cannot distract the driver they must be in crates or a harness-like seat belt. You do need to practice the crate/seat belt before you go on journeys to ensure the positive association.

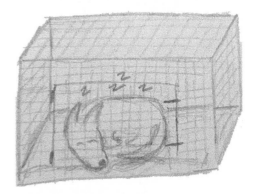

Travel Sickness

Sometimes, by following the above procedure, this may disappear as many of the symptoms were triggered by stress. However, there are animals and humans that struggle on account of the motion. We find it best to cover the crate or have darkened windows which encourage Sox to sleep. The more the crate in the car has been associated with sleep, the more likely she will sleep. It's a similar concept to rehearsing the room, which we did when introducing a dog into the household. Another dog role modelling calm behaviour and sleeping in an adjoining crate can be very helpful.

If you have a long journey, then do frequent stops. Keep her interaction calm at the rest stops, more calming games rather than high excitement games. If we play high arousal games, it will be difficult for Sox to calm down and simply accept the sleep idea. If you have had a high excitement time, then remember to transition with some calming games before asking Sox to return to the crate and expecting her to sleep.

Medication research

Lavender oil for calmness.

Maropitant Citrate is a strong anti-emetic. This is best given two hours before travel and will prevent sickness related vomiting in the majority of cases for up to a day.

Ginger works well in settling a dodgy tummy but is not as powerful as Maropitant.

Pheromones: Adaptil for dogs. These will give a feeling of wellbeing and relaxation, with a feeling of safety and reassurance. Either a spray or impregnated into the collar work well.

Calming supplements:

These can prevent additional stress from causing the travel sickness to become worse. Examples are Calmex or Zylkene.

If essential travel is required with a dog that struggles with travel sickness then the veterinarian may recommend a prescription sedative, your dog will need to be in good health, and you do need to make sure your pet is never unattended. This should only be used as a last resort.

Herbs for upset tummies: Ginger, Peppermint, Catnip, Fennel or Dill. These can be given in combination or separately.

Herbs for anxiety: Valerian, which will also calm a nervous stomach.

Mild sedative: Oatstraw, Skullcap, Passionflower, again alone or in combination.

Giving herbs: It is often best to use a tincture instead of dried herbs. The dosage depends on the dog and application, but a general rule of thumb is:

Tincture 12-30 drops per 20 pounds of bodyweight twice daily

Dried herbs – 1 teaspoon per 20 pound of body weight, sprinkled on food twice daily.

Homeopathy: Cocculus indicus, given just before getting in the car. Give 3 pellets crushed in some water or in a dropper bottle.

Anxiety: Rescue remedy, a popular flower essence

Argentum Nitricum especially when nausea is accompanies by nervousness. 3 pellets or crushed and dropped in water or dropper bottle.

Ensure you do not touch the pellet if you can help it. Best from the cap directly into Sox's mouth. Do not give the remedies with food. You can give more on the journey if felt necessary.

For homeopathy dosage does not depend on size and weight, give the same dose.

A Brief Case Study

Sox presented as being over excited generally in the house and especially on walks. A very anxious dog, who would tremble when worried. This was most noticeable when strangers approached and especially if they stroked her – or looked as if they were going to. She would also choose to frequently bark and spin on walks. She was never quiet and calm when on a walk.

Her owners, Judith and Mark, contacted us specifically regarding problems with travelling. Sox would howl and drool the moment she was in the car. If the journey was longer than ten minutes, she would often be sick and sometimes defecate. Clearly this was very unpleasant for all and had the effect of making their children feel sick too. They had a family holiday planned which involved a journey of several hours. They did not want to place Sox in kennels especially given her high anxiety levels and counting the fact that she was a rescue - albeit three years ago.

Sox was not actually underweight, but her owners were worried that she was skinny. She was not a food motivated dog and often did not eat her food. Judith often tempted her by adding tasty treats to her food with varying success.

Although we were called in to help with travel sickness it was very apparent this was just an expression of an underlying emotional condition. Sox was very anxious, pessimistic and fearful. To address the travelling issue, it was suggested that since Sox stared to drool and shake when anywhere near the car, especially if she had seen preparations for a family car journey, that the routine and feed bowl were ditched.

To build up Sox's motivation to eat, some fun, no pressure games were introduced. She loved chasing, so orientation games where food was activated were great for her. She also enjoyed seeking food, simple scent games were also employed. These were very beneficial as a calming activity too.

Once Sox was happy and confident with the games and her motivation to eat was improved, she was fed her daily allowance near the car, several times over the day. Care was taken to keep a comfortable distance for Sox. Games were varied, kept fun and no pressure, getting closer to the car. Her body language was carefully monitored to ensure she was still relaxed and confident. Then food was given in the car, keeping the doors open and leaving Sox free to choose to get in the car herself. Using similar procedures to crate training to increase duration, Sox was happy to get in the car and remain there happily chewing Kongs etc.

The next stage was to start the engine, but not travel anywhere. In the meantime, further ditching of the routine meant Sox would often wear her harness but not go anywhere. She was *no longer over excited and anxious when her harness was put on. Additional holistic options were discussed. Her owners decided to try ginger for settling the stomach and lavender for calmness.*

By ditching the routine so Sox was no longer already over threshold as soon as her harness was on and by ditching the bowl food could be used to play games for optimism and calmness Sox was now calm in the car. Journey length was gradually increased, Sox travelled in a covered crate. Rescue Remedy was used before and sometimes during a journey. Sox is now able to take a long journey. Her owners do continue to give her a break at least every two hours.

Sox now is much calmer on walks generally. The ditching of the routine and bowl and giving her daily allowance in games and calmness protocol has had a very beneficial impact on the rest of her life. Her owners are now looking at games for loose leash walking and recall, having witnessed first-hand how successful they are at tacking perceived behaviour issues.

Summary

- When training always remember baby steps and the 95% rule. If something is not working, think about why this may be and break the steps down even more. Pay attention to body language and the stress bucket. Events that happened yesterday may be impacting on today.
- Ditching the routine helps with calmness since Sox is not predicting something exciting or scary is going to happen. This is a trigger which raises the level in the stress bucket. Management of Sox's environment by ditching the routine helps her to make the choices you prefer.
- By managing the delivery of food differently you are helping meet your dog's emotional needs, remember the 7 drives we discussed in 1.1 and 1.2?

Mythbuster Moment: An adult dog needs one or two meals a day, in his own food bowl, at a specific time of day following a routine. This needs to be a commercially prepared food to ensure all his nutritional needs are met, right? Wrong. You can choose to give your dog food over the day to suit yourself, ditching the bowl and delivering the food in a variety of ways.

By doing this you are building up a tolerance of frustration, enriching your dog's life and paying in hugely to your relationship bank account.

Second Myth: Do not give your dog human food or he will steal food, pick it up off the floor when on walks and so on. Actually, you can use human food. Simply ensure you have given permission for the dog to eat it. Suitable human food such as chicken or beef etc makes very powerful rewards, much preferred over kibble.

In the next two chapters we will discuss how we can grow calmness. Remember a calm dog makes great choices.

CALMING ACTIVITIES

An introduction to crate and boundary games.

- I love my bed: encouraging duration on the boundary, bed or in the crate.
- Developing an on/off switch for arousal.

A brief testimonial of Diesel, a male Staffie/Boxer cross and Pepper, a female Labrador:

"I have two dogs and I thought one was always more stressed and reactive than the other. It was actually, probably the other way around. Diesel, my Staffie cross, was full on looking like she wanted to kill any dog we met on walks, whereas Pepper, my Labrador, used to freeze slightly and tried to get me to turn around and go home. Putting other factors together I do know now that Pepper was finding the encounter just as stressful as Diesel.

Learning more about how excitement can intensify emotions and lead to undesirable behaviour encouraged me to keep both dogs calm if they were showing anxiety. I now play the exciting games when I know they are relaxed and in a calm state of mind. It works surprisingly well. Learning about the stress bucket was a life changer. Once I knew how to empty the bucket by calming activities it was pretty instant success. Within two days I could see the difference. Both Diesel and Pepper can now enjoy their walks which means I do too. They are so relaxed at home now, it's awesome having a peaceful house now."

Calming activities.

In Chapter 1.3 we discussed how calmness is key to the welfare, health, longevity and comfort of Diesel. We discussed the calmness circle. Crates and boundaries are key to calmness if introduced and implemented with care.

Many people dislike the idea of Pepper being in a crate as it is viewed as a cage with all the associated negative beliefs and emotions. As we will explore in section 4, our thoughts and emotions directly affect Pepper's thoughts and emotions. Pepper may know her partner is not happy and is anxious when requesting she goes into the crate and so, not surprisingly, Pepper may view it with corresponding negativity, and anxiety.

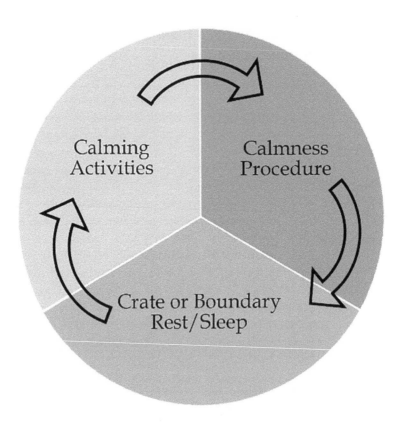

Benefits of using a crate

The crate makes life easy for Pepper to simply go to sleep. The hard work of making choices is taken away. It is a safe place, a den, a place of comfort, peace and security. It has positive associations of calmness. We like to make sure when Pepper is in her crate, nobody bothers her. This includes her canine friends and especially children. It is a place where she can sleep. Remember, dogs need 16-18 hours of sleep per day to be thoroughly rested and choose the behaviour out of the calm boxes. If they do not get enough sleep, they can be like the fractious toddler who has not had the afternoon nap.

We have many Huskies currently who have been re-homed at least once. Blade and Shadow have been rehomed twelve times in a six-month span 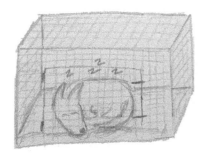 and were a day away from being euthanised. We were told they would not tolerate being in crates. They were three-and-a-half when they came to us. What's even more challenging, they are amazing escape artists and are able to trash ordinary crates with no problem. Now though, both choose to settle happily in crates. Many of the huskies we rescue have had a previous negative experience with crates as a place of punishment or deprivation. All of them now view the crate as a great place, they see an open crate door and rush to go in. They do not have their own special crate – any crate, anywhere, will do just fine. Flexibility is important.

For anybody that knows about huskies, they will know that huskies are generally good at escaping and that they have a high prey drive. So, if they do decide to open the door (often being able to open even round handled doors that open inwards) they may run off, and chase, catch and possibly kill something they see as prey. Most furry animals are on the Huskies list, whether they are sheep, deer etc. Their recall is known to be poor and their energy level high with a great desire to run. Twenty miles is nothing to them. Crates are a great way of keeping huskies (and other unsuspecting animals) safe.

We work mostly from home, having clients come for learning to do the mushing, Bikejoring or canine coaching. This means people and dogs are coming and going all day. Our guys have learned to carry on resting throughout. The hard work is convincing the humans to stay calm.

The same principles we are going to describe with boundaries apply to crates. The advantage the crate has is that you can choose to close the door. We do not close the door until the dog is perfectly happy and settled with it open, then casually close it for a few moments, drop a food treat in, or have a filled Kong or bone in there already. Later we build up the duration. It is best not to put a highly excited Pepper into a crate. Seek calmness first and then use the crates/boundaries. Once Pepper is very practiced and happy with crates then she will settle, even if she's excited. It is always a good idea to bring down the excitement as a matter of course otherwise going in the crate could be viewed as punishing and becomes frustrating. A frustrated dog is likely to choose a behaviour you do not want.

Boundary games are brilliant at developing an on/off switch to arousal (there are other games too). Boundaries are so useful in so many ways that I have included them in this chapter of calmness. They will help Pepper get the rest she needs and, provide one or two of the calmness strategies.

We will work towards the goal that, when Pepper is cued to go on the boundary, she will choose to stay calmly on her boundary (bed/crate) until given a cue as a release.

Similarly, Pepper will then opt to go on her boundary without a cue. If she does go without a cue, then she is free to come off again whenever she wants.

A boundary could be a mat, towel, platform, raised dog bed, ordinary dog bed, piece of cardboard – in fact anything can be a boundary. This means eventually Pepper sees lots of opportunities to play boundary games and feel like she knows the game/rules as well as feeling safe, happy and calm on her boundary. Cueing for a boundary also means that Pepper has a job to do which can help take away the confusion of too much choice.

As with all games and training, it is best to start at home when Pepper is already calm and in a receptive, learning mindset.

Benefits of Boundary games

Boundary games create impulse control. They can decrease arousal and help to promote calmness. They can balance and level out arousal as needed, enhance your relationship, and even boost motivation. They can help to prevent jumping, counter surfing (attempting to steal from your kitchen side) and improve recall. They will impact in a hugely beneficial way in all aspects of your life with Pepper. Make boundary games your number one game.

Goals:

- Go to this area on cue. (you choose – is it a dog bed, mat, crate, towel)
- Be calm and remain until the release cue. Upon release interact with partner first – play other games etc.
- Pepper loving her boundary/bed/crate, choosing it and resting quietly. Peacefully snoozing.

The How-To:

1. Shape the value of the bed. Reward any positive interaction (even just looking) with the bed. This is very much the starting point with a dog who has previously had a poor experience. You may take longer at all these stages.
2. Reward the choice to go on the bed (do not use a leash). If they go to their boundary of their own accord, simply give them a treat.
3. When Pepper is on the bed feed lots of rewards. Make sure you place the food calmly onto the bed, not to the mouth. You want the value in the boundary/bed, and you want calmness. Ensure you role model calmness.
4. Slow down the rate of feeding to the bed… And then slow down some more.
5. Throw a piece of food away from the bed and use a word you intend to use for your release from the bed. Say the release word a second or two before throwing the food so the release cue becomes powerful too.

6. If Pepper chooses to go back on the bed reward generously but, do not give a cue yet to go on the bed. Your position is important, often if the bed is in between you and Pepper she will choose to jump onto the bed.

    Build the value and don't forget release cue. Popular release cues are 'break' or 'free.'

Adding Duration

7. When Pepper offers to sit or lie down then generously reward this. We are building relaxation.
8. Increase and decrease duration from three seconds to ten seconds then five seconds, seven seconds, two seconds etc. Mix it up, don't make it harder and harder because that is not fun for Pepper and becomes stressful.

Note: Whenever training, don't just keep making it harder and harder as Pepper is learning. Throw in some very easy wins, keep it fun, no pressure.

9. If Pepper leaves without the cue, don't put pressure on her. Remember it is a fun game and not discipline, simply hold her collar or harness for a few seconds, then allow her back on and reward the choice to go back on.
10. We need to be aware of feeding slowly to the bed to keep things interesting and fun. To increase anticipation, you can fiddle with the food before placing onto the bed. Remember anticipation is motivating.
11. You are teaching your dog to do nothing and be calm.
12. Keep giving value to the release cue – and don't forget to release.

A Brief Case Study

David contacted us as Diesel's behaviour on a walk was causing he and Shelly a considerable amount of embarrassment, frustration and anxiety. Other dog walkers and passers-by were making comments such as 'you need to socialise your dog', 'you should put a muzzle on that dog'. Shelly felt she could not walk the dogs by herself and David sometimes worked away from home for a few days. The situation was getting worse with Diesel's reactivity escalating.

During the consultation is became apparent that both dogs were of a pessimistic mind set, lacking confidence and were showing anxiety in other aspects of their life not just on walks. They were getting very little rest as they were both exhibiting high levels of vigilance. Calming activities were discussed and introduced. Both dogs had used crates as puppies and were happy to eat and chew Kongs. Shelley initially was uncomfortable with the idea of utilising a crate. It was decided that David would do the initial re-introduction to the crates as he was comfortable with the idea. Almost immediately David and Shelly reported how much calmer and happier both dogs were. They were no longer reacting to any noise and were sleeping twice as many hours as before.

Although David and Shelly expressed concern about not going for the twice daily walks for a few days, they did try it. They were given demonstrations for the games that could be played for exercise in the garden with a focus on maintaining calmness. Scent games were heavily utilised. This gave the necessary time for the stress buckets to empty.

Games for confidence and optimism were introduced. David and Shelly were encouraged to go on quiet walks where they would be unlikely to meet other dogs for a few weeks. Then gradually increasing the likelihood of meeting other dogs but being able to keep a comfortable distance and simply keep their dogs engaged with them by playing the well-rehearsed games.

David and Shelley now have the knowledge to keep both dogs stress bucket empty using calming activities. By playing games for optimism both dogs are now less fearful, they are generally calm and happy. With these methods, they can now walk both dogs comfortably.

Summary

- In this chapter we have discussed how to train your dog to love their bed, to choose to lie quietly and rest. For extra safety and security crate training has been described at length, with the goal of your dog loving the crate.
- There are so many other benefits from crate training, calm travel, being able to visit anywhere, put up the crate and know your dog will settle and is safe even if you need to leave him unattended. This gives you so much freedom without guilt as you know he is safe, calm and happy.
- Crate and boundary games can help develop the on/off switch – chewing a Kong in the crate helps to bring arousal level down quickly. The boundaries become associated with calming activities, so being on a boundary helps your dog to come down from excitement to calm.

Mythbuster Moment: It is cruel to put your dog in a cage.

In reality, true crate training teaches your dog to love their crate, to choose to go in. To know they are safe and can sleep without worry. It is your job to ensure you build up the desire to go in the crate and remain calmly and happily.

In the next chapter we will introduce other activities which will help you enrich your dog's life whilst also growing calmness.

PROMOTING CALMNESS

CHAPTER INTRODUCTION:

Calming games. The calmness procedure.

- Scatter feeding.
- Reward nothing.
- Circles, Figure Eights and Serpentines (Wombling) Games
- 'It's Raining Treats'.
- Boundary games, taking the boundary outside.
- Benefits of massage for calming.
- Cone game/harness and leash training.

A brief testimonial of Nova, a female Northern Inuit.

"I just loved playing the games, especially the calmness games. I found using circling, serpentines worked brilliantly. It is something I can do pretty well anywhere whenever I feel it necessary. As suggested, I mix it up with some scatter feeding, some 'reward nothing' and gentle stroking. It's so simple, but transformational. Nova, my Northern Inuit, and I enjoy loose leash walks now. If she starts to pull, we do some 'treats from the sky' and maybe change direction. So many options to keep things interesting but calm. Knowing I have the techniques gives me confidence to go out with Nova. I used to ask my son to walk her which could sometimes cause an argument."

We know we keep talking about calmness, but it truly is the key to your success. We have, therefore, devoted a chapter to helping you achieve calmness.

The failsafe, and stand-by, is the calmness triad: calmness procedure with actively rewarding calm. We have previously introduced this idea with crate and boundary games (chapter 2.3): Licking and chewing bones, long lasting chews, puzzle toys, food filled Kongs, and encouraging as much sleep as possible by the provision of safe places and places away from busy and noisy areas of the house to be associated with rest and sleep.

General principle for calmness: When working for calmness slow your movements down, keep the food rewards relatively low value (high value may excite too much), keep the delivery of the food slow and calm and avoid too much animation. Speak in more soothing tones

Games for calmness:
Doing Nothing is Perfect

This is a similar exercise to the work you have done with boundary and crate training where you reward calmness or when the dog is literally doing nothing. Nothing is good.

Prepare eight low value treats (as low as you feel will still interest your dog but not excite). Sit in front of Nova, watch her closely whenever she stops moving (even for a second) and reward. When she is still again reward again. You are capturing the time when she relaxes her muscles and brings her energy down and does nothing. She receives the treat by staying still. Once understood and mastered this is a very powerful game.

Advantages of Doing Nothing is Perfect:

It helps to return to low arousal after Nova has been in high arousal, returning the capacity to think and make better choices. It creates a good transition in preparation for going in a crate after exercise or playing higher energy games and is great for easily aroused, frustrated dogs or those with a lack of impulse control. Even dogs that are anxious, reactive dogs or dogs that lack in confidence.

Doing 'Nothing is Perfect' is hugely beneficial as it can be used anywhere. Remember to have this perfected at home before taking it to more challenging environments. This game can help to diffuse situations where Nova is predicting something exciting, and is in danger of becoming over aroused, and losing her capacity to think, and make good choices.

Circles, serpentines and Figure of eight
walking (Wombling Games)

Any horse trainer will instantly recognise that doing shapes will help to calm a horse whilst providing gymnastic benefits. Remember that you are

training the dog in front of you. Many people believe that the more repetitions, the more calming the effect. However, one horse, Lucy, thought
otherwise. She found it stimulating and wanted to go faster and faster,
no matter how small the circles. She was incredibly agile and enjoyed the
movements. With her, frequent changes of directions helped. She then had
to engage her brain and not simply predict.

These are such simple exercises, but very powerful and are best performed with a collar and harness, or harness with a front and back clip together with a double ended leash or two leads. One clip on the front of the
harness or collar and the other on the back ring of the harness.

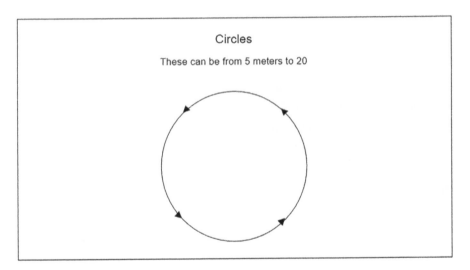

Simply walk a circle in either direction until Nova settles. The size of
the circle is up to you and the room available. It is best not to be too large,
though you can vary the size. You can spiral in and out while varying the
pace to keep attention on you. You can practice with Nova on the inside of
the circle and the outside. Often Nova will be calmer with you on the outer
circle, maybe in between her and the distracting environment. Simply look

where you intend to go and keep your mental focus on Nova. Encourage her focus to be on you. You can deliver some treats, but this will need some practice for the mechanics given the fact that you are handling the leashes as well. Treat giving can sometimes interfere with the focused, meditative state you are striving for.

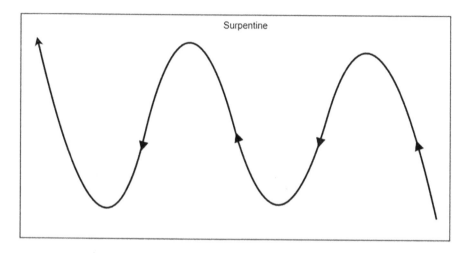

Surpentine

You can change direction on the curve by doing serpentine movements. You could walk around a car park doing small circles in the corners or even along the sides.

These exercises help with calmness, and loose leash walking.

For figure-eight walking, initially, it can be useful to put up two markers or obstacles to give you focus and direction. Then, walk a figure of eight so each marker is within one of your circles. You can simply repeat the figure eight. Equally, you can choose to remain circling for a while and then move on to the opposite direction circle. Remember to vary your speed to help keep focus on you.

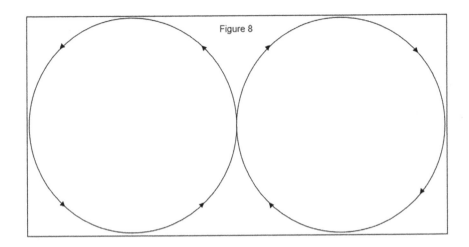

Figure 8

'It's Raining Treats' - Keep your eye on the hand

Firstly (and this may take a while) teach Nova to catch treats. To set up for success initially use treat that are very easy to see, consider their colour and size. Position your hand above Nova's nose (this will depend on the size of your dog for distance) and release a treat. Initially, Nova may not catch the treat, but you will praise the attempt and allow her to eat it off the floor.

As dogs like to be efficient and find the fastest way to get the treat, they will keep attempting eventually succeeding with the catch. Have a party when they do so. Only do between six and ten repetitions before moving on to another game. You can always return to this one. Even if she is unable to catch the treat, there will be concentration and focus on your hand. For while Nova is concentrating and using her brain, she is keeping calm. Like all other games we work on it at home, and then in more distracting environments. As Nova becomes more practiced, she will be able to catch, even in more challenging environments. Remember the Yerkes-Dodson curve from chapter 1.3?

Boundary games

This is an extension of the games discussed in the last few chapters. You can suggest new boundaries by your position and intention. Try placing your chosen boundary, we'll say a towel, in front of you. Nova will have built up value orienting and coming to you, usually because sitting or standing in front of you has a history of reward.

It is hard to resist those eyes looking hopefully at you, so we generally interact, perhaps with a treat. Nova is likely to stand or sit on the towel, reward. You can then gradually build up the game, position yourself so that the boundary is on your right side, left side or even behind you. This encourages Nova to problem solve and increases her flexibility.

> Note: Make one change at a time. Keep it easy and set Nova up for success. This applies to all situations not just boundary games.
>
> We may use a familiar boundary, in a familiar environment and only change our own position. Or, new boundary, familiar position, familiar environment. Alternatively, familiar environment, familiar position, unfamiliar boundary.
>
> Keep it easy to set up for success. As your partnership develops, together with Nova's confidence and skill set, you may be able to change two aspects.

It is important is to ensure Nova's stress bucket is well below threshold and that she is able to think. We keep games short and fun with no pressure.

As always, set up at home using multiple boundaries for flexibility. You can choose anything to be a boundary, often Nova will choose her own boundaries as she understands the concept. After playing in the house, play the boundary game in your garden, then in quiet areas out in the environment where there are not too many distractions. You can choose anything to be a boundary on your walk: a wall, a tree stump, be creative.

You can mix up these games, do some figure of eight then move on to, serpentines, boundary games, a little 'It's Raining Treats', the circles etc. After the games try some scatter feeding to relax her. Perhaps a short scent game? We go into those later in the book.

By utilising this multiple game approach and keeping each game very short, you can enter more distracting environments. You will be able to keep Nova's focus on you, in a calm, thoughtful way.

In the early days of introducing Nova to the household and walks, it is very important to keep the focus on calm. This can help set the precedent and expectation. You can add some higher arousal, fun games later. You are likely to have played higher arousal games with any previous dogs, for example fetch and tug. Hold back on those for the first week or so. Longer if necessary.

When you do introduce games with higher excitement (chapter 3.4), ensure you follow a high arousal game with a calming one to help build up a good 'off switch'. As we do this, we are helping to get a bigger hole in the stress bucket. We're using a cycle of high excitement to calm to high excitement to calm etc.

Put your Nose in it Game

Many rescue dogs become very excited or anxious when they see the preparation for going on a walk. Check out the travel advice we gave in chapter 2.2, the principles are the same.

If there are previous negative associations with collars and harness etc, then the 'Put your Nose' in it game is a great way to change this. You may have tried giving treats when putting on a harness and found that it does not work as effectively as you anticipated in changing their mindset to a positive association. It needs to be broken up into baby steps with Nova choosing the next step herself. This gives her the feeling of control, which helps enormously with her confidence.

Find something that Nova can place her nose into. You can utilise lots of objects to generalise this concept. Children's toys are good. Initially, simply looking at your chosen object/toy will result in a treat, then coming closer, then putting nose in. Remember to be calm and put no pressure on her.

You can progress, use the leash and give rewards when a previously fearful Nova interacts with it. Build up to putting her head over the leash, held between your two hands. Then make a loop out of the leash, this needs to be easy for Nova to place her head through. Reward her when she does. We're not using a cue because we want it to be her choice. She needs to feel she is in control.

As she becomes more enthusiastic and confident you can switch to collars and harnesses. Initially, use a harness that is too large, so it is very easy for Nova to put her head through. Be generous with the food reward when her head is through, then remove the neck loop and don't feed. Then offer the neck loop again, and if Nova puts her head through, generous rewards again. This leads to being keen to push the head through the neck loop. Do not be in a hurry to clip the harness in place. If Nova is happy you may clip and unclip a few times, then remove to get her used to it.

Be aware that the sound of the clip may have negative associations so you can do similar baby steps, separately away from the harness and leash work, simply using the clip in positive settings when you know Nova is calm.

Remember the principle of only changing one thing at once? Baby steps. 95% rule.

Practice putting the collar, harness or leash on at home when Nova is calm and then simply use the 'Nothing is Perfect' game, give a chew or any of the other calming activities. It is best Nova does not associate the harness, leash or collar with high energy. Otherwise, before you have gone out the door, she will be in a state of high arousal and will find it difficult to listen to you. She may even choose behaviours you do not wish for.

This means you will ditch the routine of putting a leash on and heading out for a walk. Put the harness and leash on then sit down for a coffee. Put it on and off several times. It is a good idea to vary the times of the walk. Remember you want to avoid the anticipation that comes from predictability. Be creative.

Massage

Massage is very beneficial for health and wellbeing. Performed correctly it lowers heart rate, blood pressure, improves circulation, facilitates the removal of toxins, and can help ease tension. If done for this purpose it also promotes relaxation. You can choose to learn more about how to massage Nova for all the above health benefits or simply choose to use it as a relaxation and relationship enhancing tool. Remember for this to be valuable Nova needs to enjoy your touch. Pay close attention to her body language, your intuition and the smallest sign. Always allow her to move away and finish the session when she chooses.

It is important that, if you intend to use massage as a calming activity, you choose a quiet place. You may need to use a transition activity e.g. chews or scatter feeding to bring Nova's energy down so she can relax and accept the massage. If she moves away from your touch allow her to. Do not insist. Maybe wait and invite her to return – no pressure, no expectation.

Often, it works well to wait until Nova is settled next to you and then initiate contact on an area you know she generally enjoys. Use slow, steady movements, follow your intuition and watch carefully to see if she remains relaxed or becomes even more relaxed. Only stroke areas she is comfortable with you doing so. If you know she enjoys particular scents e.g. lavender, you can put some on your hands. We will go into a little more detail on oils etc in section 4. Use long, slow strokes starting from Nova's neck, along her body towards the tail in the direction of the coat. The soothing re-petitive movements will help to relax her alongside the beneficial action of touch. Remember the social bonding drive, nurturing, release of oxytocin feel-good chemicals? Ten minutes of your full, heart centred attention and touch will have a huge impact on even the most attention seeking of dogs.

In addition to the above, you can utilise aromatherapy. Perhaps use room diffusers or more direct application. It is essential to use good quality oils and not the synthetic versions on the shelves of general stores. The correct application is discussed with the usual proviso to allow Nova to choose what she needs.

Animals naturally want to return to balance (homeostasis) and are likely to know what they need to do so. Be aware they can make poor choices too especially with regard to diet.

Music

Equally, for relaxation you can make use of carefully chosen music. Many studies have been performed which reveal beneficial effects on dogs in a kennel situation. This includes working dogs and rescue homes. Classical music has been shown to have good results and there are even music tracks you can purchase compiled especially for dogs.

We will discuss further touching techniques for health and wellbeing in chapter 4.4. This will include the important bladder meridian and a brief introduction to some acupressure points.

As always, you can build up by baby steps and eventually have Nova hap-py with touch in previously sensitive areas. Massaging areas such as paws can be introduced more as a training exercise (using counter conditions and desensitisation techniques) rather than for relaxation. Once Nova is very happy with paws being touched then paw massage can be slowly introduced with brilliant results and will be relaxing too.

A Brief Case Study

Janice contacted us as she was having difficulty walking her Northern Innuit. Nova had pulled her over four times and had caused rope burn which resulted in Janice letting go of the leash. Nova ran off and it took two hours to find her. Sadly, she had run to a nature reserve and killed several ducks. Since then Janice did not feel confident to take Nova on walks, relying on her twenty-year-old son. Her son was not always willing or available to take Nova out (although he was the person who wanted

this breed of dog). Nova came to them at eight weeks old. Although some things are easier now, her size, strength and high prey drive have resulted in the consideration of re-homing. The son, Dave, is shortly to join Her Majesty's Armed Forces so Janice will have sole care of Nova.

During the consultation it was discovered that Nova was not very attentive to Janice, ignoring requests to recall from the garden, generally not being attentive. This meant there was no connection at all when out on walks as the environment was always more interesting than Janice in Nova's opinion.

Nova was a confident, optimistic dog, happy to meet people and other dogs but she did become excited and too strong for Janice to control effectively. She was happy and calm in the house and garden, getting plenty of sleep and rest times.

It was decided to focus on boosting the relationship at home first. The bowl was ditched, and calming games practiced. These were playing in the garden initially to gain the skill and raise the level of trust and confidence. Scatter feeding was a favourite as Janice could then distract Nova from pulling towards a chosen target. Circles and figures of eight were extremely helpful to keep a focus and build cooperation. 'It's Raining Treats' was valuable in keeping Nova's attention if Janice saw something in the distance that she felt may be a challenge.

Janice also focused on boundary games, she built up huge value for Nova choosing to sit on a towel that would accompany them on their walks. She only needed to put the towel on the floor and Nova would choose to sit on it. Janice could then give very slow delivery of food and wait for the hazard to go by.

Using the cone game, Nova was also introduced to a head halter. Previously that had been tried but Nova showed she disliked it and would remove it. Nova is now comfortable with using the head halter which give Janice the confidence to know she can control Nova. Janice uses the head halter in busy environments where she needs close control, then she removes it and uses a walking belt, long line and harness with a back clip in quiet locations. Using this equipment

Nova and Janice can play other games to keep building up a more positive relationship so Nova chooses proximity.

Janice and Nova now have a very positive relationship and Janice. feels she has the necessary skills to walk Nova with confidence.

Summary

- Knowing how to keep your dog calm, ensure he has plenty of enrichment activities by ditching the bowl and routine means you are well on the way to providing the perfect forever home.
- You are taking control of the environment and managing your household, keeping everybody safe, calm and happy.

Mythbuster Moment: My dog is too strong for me to walk so I cannot exercise him.

Not only can you play games in the safety of your house and garden, but you can train for loose leash walking, so you do not need strength. The games will enrich his life and meet his emotional needs. In the next chapter you will learn some other games which can create more excitement, you already know how to lower excitement and create calm.

Second Myth: You can't teach an old dog new tricks.

Yes, you can teach an old dog new tricks, keep reading. These fun games and techniques apply to all breeds of dogs and all ages.

In the previous chapters we have discussed how powerful emotions are and how they drive behaviour, we have learnt how important managing stress levels are if we want our dog to choose the behaviour we want. We now know that calmness and plenty of sleep is essential to keeping the stress level well below threshold. There are plenty of techniques to achieve the calmness we need.

In the next section we are going to concentrate on power boosting your partnership, creating the dog that chooses you over the environment. If you have been struggling with loose leash walking and recall, this is for you.

PART 3

POWERFUL
PARTNERSHIP

CONSIDERING YOUR
DOG'S PERSONALITY

CHAPTER INTRODUCTION:

Considering your dog's personality, genetics
(breed influence), previous learning and behaviour habits.

- Train the dog in front of you.
- Personality types: Optimist and Pessimist dogs.
- Tolerance of frustration.
- Flexibility.
- Are they a thinker or a doer?

Take into account your dog's breed and propensity to a certain type of behaviour whilst remembering that each dog is an individual. It is likely to be a little more difficult to train a recall to a dog originally bred to hunt and chase when she has her prey in sight.

Whilst noting the breed, do guard against labelling and assuming you will never be able to achieve certain behaviours simply because of the breed. They are all individual, train the dog in front of you. High energy working dogs can find life in an urban setting frustrating.

A brief testimonial of Rosie, a female Jack Russel.

"When I learned more about what Jack Russel's were originally bred for, I realised that she was simple showing the behaviour typical of a Jack Russel. Sometimes she got so stupidly stubborn and I'd get frustrated. Finding out that, in other situations, she'd have been a prized dog for her determination and toughness was a bit of an eye opener.

Learning more about their personalities, how it affects behaviour and how it can be changed has been fascinating. I think I have bored all my friends and family talking about how games can help change personality. Rosie is much more flexible and optimistic now which means she no longer feels the need to charge at the fence at all passing dogs or people. The most valuable lesson I've learned, is that while it may be harder to get her to recall from something that was bred to chase it can still be done. I've reached the point that we have a consistent recall and far less barking. Something of a relief for me."

Train the dog in front of you

Although we will discuss general breed characteristics which can help you to understand your individual dog's needs, be aware that there are huge variations of drive and personality within a breed.

Whilst it is helpful to know why your dog is doing something it is equally important not to make assumptions that because you have a specific breed you will be unable train under some circumstances. For example, with a hunting dog you may assume you will not be able to call it off the chase. It may be more difficult, even take longer, but it is doable if you follow the steps and play the games. The 95% rule is of paramount importance.

Earlier in the book we discussed small stress buckets and small holes in the bucket – this is where individual personality comes in. Some dogs are very sensitive, easily stressed and find life more challenging. Just the same with people. Studies demonstrate that some babies are born with a more reactive temperament. Additionally, think back to chapter 1.2 where we discussed how the stress of the mum during pregnancy can have detrimental effects on her pups. The interaction between environmental and genetic effects is complicated. Simply train the dog in front of you being aware of context.

We aim to discuss personality in terms of confidence or anxiety, optimism or pessimism, easily frustrated or able to deal with frustration, flexible or inflexible. A thinker or a doer.

The games we will introduce in the next two chapters will help to develop the personality. Rosie will become more able to cope with our challenging human world successfully. Depending on the personality, and drive, you will choose to play some games more than others to help you overcome your struggles.

Although the dog is 'man's best friend', and as such the subject of much observation and scientific study, a great mystery still surrounds her origin. Some authorities put the domestication of the dog as 15,000 years ago. It is believed that it may have been the first species to be domesticated.

The huge variations between breeds can be explained by the theory that the dog was domesticated in several parts of the world at around the same time; different peoples practised selective breeding with these early domestic dogs, but with very different ends in mind.

7,500-year-old pottery shows a Greyhound/Saluki type dog bred to chase game in the desert. By 2000BC the Egyptians had mastered the principles of breeding and developed it to a high level of sophistication. Several breeds are depicted, and these include a toy dog, similar to a Maltese, bred almost certainly as a pet and not for any practical purpose.

Sculptures from Babylon, 2000BC, show dogs very similar to modern Mastiffs. It seems these were trained to fight in battle, as well as being used for hunting. The use of dogs in this way spread later on to Europe, where it is reported that dogs were used against the invading Romans in 55BC. The Romans had separate descriptive names for house dogs, shepherd dogs, sporting dogs, war dogs, dogs that would fight as a spectacle, dogs which hunted by scent, and those which hunted by sight.

Today, we have a wider range of breeds, both ancient and modern. It is important to study carefully the history of any breed you are thinking of choosing as a pet to ensure that it fits into your lifestyle. Only in the last hundred years or so have dogs evolved away from their working ancestries to become primarily companion animals. For some breeds, this transition has been more difficult than others.

During more recent years, there has been growing concern about the temperament of some breeds, with Rottweilers in particular gaining a bad reputation in the media for their ferocity. This breed has a long history as a brave and powerful guard dog and has retained some potentially aggressive traits within its personality. A Rottweiler is sometimes employed as a police dog, emphasising the responsive and intelligent side of its nature. Pit bulls (a dog bred for fighting) are in some countries a banned breed.

Other dogs, bred primarily for hunting purposes, are much harder to train successfully. Hounds such as Afghan are likely to be harder than members of the retriever group. Throughout their existence, the retriever breeds have worked closely alongside their owners. It is no coincidence that while still fulfilling their traditional role as gun dogs, retrievers are also now used as guide dogs for the blind and as assistance dogs. Their excellent scenting abilities means they can also be trained successfully to detect drugs and explosives.

Working sheepdogs can still be found throughout the world and they make popular companions, although these dogs may sometimes become rather bored and frustrated in urban surroundings. It is important to consider the individual needs of the breed, together, with your own personal surrounding and lifestyle before making any decision about choice of dog.

We work mainly with Northern Sled dogs, especially the Siberian Husky. These are thought to be one of the most ancient breeds of dogs. They were bred for incredible feats of endurance and strength on very little food, to be able to share family accommodation and to help keep each other warm in extreme cold weather, -30°C or even below. They were often free in the warmer months, when they were not needed for transport, to survive independently (without humans) by scavenging and hunting. Their tough minded, independent thinking and hunting abilities were necessary for survival. No surprise then that they may find it harder to fit the human idea of a companion dog.

Our passion is to give you the tools so you can provide the best forever-home for whatever breed of dog you welcome into your house. We work primarily with rescue huskies, most of which have had multiple homes. One pair had twelve homes in as short a span of time as six months and were due to be euthanised. We find it sad that much of the rehoming could have been avoided with the correct approach when it came to these dogs.

Even within the same litter the pups are likely to have very different personalities, some pessimistic, some very sensitive or reactive, some able to deal with frustration and so on. Perhaps some of them are oozing confidence and others not so much. From earlier discussion you know that the health and stress level of the mum will impact on the pup's personality and wellbeing. Mum's personality will have an impact both in terms of her genes and her behaviour. A bitch who had a poor start or poor nurturing as a pup is likely treat her litter in a similar way. This can result in more independent pups with a lower bonding/love drive. Early sensitive and regular handling by humans can mitigate this.

Previous learning and behaviour habits

We have, very briefly, discussed the genetic influence on Rosie, now consider previous learning and any habits your rescue dog has picked up. With your rescue dog you are unlikely to have the full story of the parental background and previous experience. Whilst this knowledge can be useful, it is more important to simply learn about your dog's personality and needs. It is often best not to simply categorise Rosie as a specific breed, or give the label of, a rescue dog. Both are labels that predispose us to think in a specific way, this may impair or prevent progress.

Initially, the behaviour a dog chooses might be random but as she gets older, she experiences more emotions and responds accordingly. She will select behaviours that she has found to be most effective when she has been in the same, or similar situations. Rosie will come with her own specific personality, probably in a state of high stress and with a way of coping with the world that she finds effective or rewarding.

Many of Rosie's behaviours may not be the ones you wish for. One example of this may be choosing a behaviour which reduces her negative feelings of fear/anxiety whether that is lunging, spinning or barking. These are the learned coping strategies. These are the ones that tend to be chosen by the active copers, whereas 'shutting down' also shows over-arousal and stress, this coping strategy is chosen by a more passive dog. Where Rosie has 'given up' may be a form of learned helplessness. This could be when Rosie has learned that in the past, she has not been able to avoid unpleasant things and now does not even try. Sadly, though, the negative emotion associated with the situation is still there. Studies have shown that dogs with a more active coping mechanism of 'being reactive' often have less cortisol in the system than the ones that show less reactivity but are quietly suffering.

Optimistic or Pessimistic personality

Scientific studies on judgement bias or optimism have been performed on many species. These are thought to be intrinsic characteristics, within the personality, of the individual animal. In a survival context, animals that are more pessimistic may take fewer risks, live longer, reproduce and protect their young very effectively which leads to the perpetuation of this characteristic. Such animals are on alert, this pays off because it means they spot the danger sooner and survive. However, in the domestic setting the optimistic dogs who are confident learn readily and are not overcome by struggles and are less easily worried by events are the ones that thrive.

The pessimistic dog as a companion animal or sports dog is generally not ideal. Because of the mentality of expecting the worst, they will be more stressed, worried, predicting more negative events and are likely to give up when faced with challenges they find hard. It is very easy to put too much pressure on a pessimistic and reactive (sensitive) dog. This is something to be very aware of when playing the games or indeed with any interaction. Training is 24/7 not just the time you think it's the 'right time to train Rosie'.

A very reactive, high energy, sensitive dog can be the very one that achieves the top places in sport or most valued as a working dog. One of our horses, Rapport, is very sensitive, spooks (anxious and vigilant) and has incredible energy levels. Not an easy horse by any means. He has, however, reached the top in endurance riding being capable of doing a hundred miles in a day, without fatigue, and being ready to go out again the next day. Ghost, a Siberian husky, is very sensitive, low in confidence but is awesome as a sled dog. He is a cuddle bunny too.

Humans too tend to be inherently optimistic or pessimistic. The good news is both human and dog can be helped to change from pessimistic to much more optimistic. It will be no surprise to know that it is easier to change Rosie. The human needs to be motivated to change.

<u>The dog optimism-pessimism test (try it at home):</u>

1. Place a bowl in one of two locations in either corner of a room
2. When the bowl is in one location (positive), there is a high value treat in it.
3. When the bowl is in the other location (negative) it is empty.
4. Rosie is kept behind a screen on the other side of the room (approximately twelve feet if possible) and then released.
5. Rosie soon learns that one location is a good thing, e.g. the bowl placed in the positive position.
6. Once Rosie goes to the bowl on the left when released the judgment bias test can start.
7. The bowl is then placed in varying positions between the positive and the negative side
8. The very pessimistic Rosie will not approach the bowl even if not far from the positive position because she assumes it is empty. The very optimistic Rosie may check it out – ever hopeful.
9. If you observe Rosie's everyday behaviour you will be able to judge her outlook on life.

Optimism Test

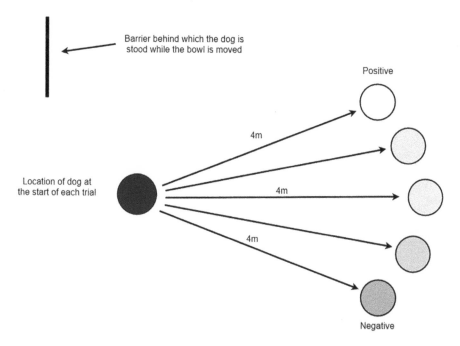

Barrier behind which the dog is stood while the bowl is moved

Positive

4m

Location of dog at the start of each trial

4m

4m

4m

Negative

Other indicators of optimism or pessimism:

A pessimistic outlook leads to many events, whether new, ambiguous or slightly strange, being perceived as being scary. Pessimistic Rosie's bucket is likely to be fairly full, given the negative reaction to a wide range of small triggers. Given such a range of triggers, any one of them may be the final one that tips Rosie to over threshold. This can be confusing because maybe yesterday Rosie met that trigger with a less full bucket and seemed ok but today, she reacts. This gives Rosie the label of unpredictable. In fact, with greater knowledge, observation, and sensitivity it is completely predictable.

Event:	An optimist:	A Pessimist:
Presented with an unusual object in the middle of the room.	May not change behavior and carry on, or they may assess the object before moving on.	May show avoidance of the object, change their behavior or implement a coping strategy such as sniffing the ground.
A usual object has moved place in the room. (E.g. a lamp or chair)	May not change behavior and carry on, or they may assess the object before moving on.	May show avoidance of the object, change their behavior or implement a coping strategy such as sniffing the ground.
During a training session, your dog offers a behavior in response to a cue or in a shaping session and you remain unresponsive or ambiguous for a few seconds.	May try the same thing again or try something new.	May leave you or implement a coping strategy like sniffing, itching etc. May struggle to try again.
A dog freezes or gives another ambiguous signal.	May move on or try an alternative behavior.	May become worried and react.
A person behaves, is dressed or adopts a posture or outline that is unusual.	May not change behavior and carry on or may assess them and then move on.	May become worried and react.

If a pessimist is worked on using optimism games, then the previous small triggers will not have that effect and the bucket stays empty. Rosie is further away from threshold in this case and is less likely to go over threshold, showing the unwanted behaviour. Of equal importance, Rosie is so much happier when not experiencing the negative emotion.

It can be that Rosie has a specific trigger which, even with an empty bucket, sends her over threshold. This is resolved by desensitization, habituation – counter conditioning. These are conditioning/training techniques that focus on a specific situation such as the trigger that sends Rosie over threshold even when her bucket is empty. It will be no surprise by now that it will be baby steps. Re-read the travel section for ideas. You will start where Rosie is still comfortable with the trigger.

For our example we'll say that Rosie is reactive when she sees another dog. In this case, find the distance that Rosie can see the other dog without reacting. Build up positive associations with that such as food. Gradually decrease the distance, paying attention throughout, and checking she remains relaxed. Even better, utilise the calming games to speed up the process. The wombling games would be ideal as you can keep Rosie's paws moving, keep her focus on you instead of the other dog. If she is staring at the other dog, you are too close, give more distance.

Tolerance of Frustration

It is often difficult to tell if Rosie is anxious, over-aroused or frustrated. The behaviour may be the same for each of them, be it barking, spinning and lunging. We must realise that the emotion driving the behaviour is different. It is good if you can tell the difference between frustration and anxiety, since we choose to tackle the emotionally anxious dog with a different strategy to a frustrated dog. If you are unsure simply default to calm, choose a transitioning calming game. There are many games to play to build up tolerance of frustration.

Building the tolerance of frustration helps to enhance learning as Rosie is more able to cope with failure and try again. If you are too slow with the reward Rosie can still cope and be patient. Importantly, it means Rosie can cope with changes to her routine and expectations easily.

If Rosie has poor tolerance of frustration then she is likely to give up in a training session or is reluctant to try new choices, she fails to think through a struggle. She is likely to show her frustration by other activities such as zoomies, sniffing or even biting.

Frustration is a negative emotion, together with a high arousal it can trigger the fear response. Look back to Bob's mood circle in chapter 1.3. If we can improve the tolerance of frustration then Rosie can remain calm and be in 'happy land', if high arousal via an exciting game is played now then Rosie remains in happy land.

Life is not predictable so best for Rosie to be prepared for this and learns the skills to able to cope.

You may recognise this character trait and have maybe referred to Rosie as 'impatient' if she becomes reactive or perhaps 'stubborn' if she is a passive coper 'shuts down' or gives up and wants to leave the situation.

To build up the tolerance as always baby steps. Set up situations where something desirable is not immediately accessible but if Rosie makes the choices you want then it becomes available. Keep this very easy at the start and then more difficult. Do remember though to give some easy wins and not to simply go more and more difficult.

Flexibility

If Rosie always responds to the same situation in the same way, then she likely lacks flexibility. A flexible response to the same situation can be very useful. If we want to teach a different response, then we need to train flexibility. If, for example, Rosie usually barks at other dogs and you want her to check in with you instead. You need to teach her that other responses are possible and that she can choose a different strategy. For each time Rosie performs a certain behaviour in the same situation, the connection becomes stronger and stronger. Sometimes we may want this, often we don't. It is very powerful to develop a problem-solving Rosie, who looks for other ways to solve a problem or cope with a struggle. We need to develop this flexibility too.

A Thinker or a Doer? Active or Passive personality.

A thinker is likely to go still in a new situation, she likes to understand new rules, she needs lower arousal in order to learn. Once they have understanding and become more confident then they add speed. Thinkers are likely to seem hesitant. You need to work out how to adapt your expectations to suit your dog. If you are more of a doer and like to move quickly, then it is easy to become frustrated with Rosie if she is a thinker.

The Doer or Active coper will prefer movement, they are likely to offer greater speed and intensity when learning, they operate at a high level of arousal.

B F Skinner in 1973 stated that, "it is the teacher's function to contrive conditions under which students learn. It is your job to create the conditions under which the student can learn."

The games and their relevance to a future usefulness need not be obvious. If the advice for ditching the bowl and routine seems to have no relevance to poor recall then simply remember, we are contriving the conditions under which Rosie can learn.

All the strategies you are employing, ditch the bowl, ditch the routine, playing seemingly irrelevant and bizarre games are creating the conditions under which Rosie can learn. It can seem as if you had one or two main struggles and expected a more direct approach. But, if we only address the behaviour and not the underlying emotion, then a different, yet equally undesirable behaviour is likely to arise. If you were working directly on barking and you inhibit the behaviour. Perhaps by punishment. They will probably choose another behaviour such as nipping or biting because the underlying emotion is still there. This is not a desirable outcome. It's far better to work on the underlying emotions and have a calm and happy Rosie who can now feel comfortable in situations she used to find a struggle.

A Brief Case Study

Jill arranged a consultation for Rosie as she was concerned that Rosie was very noisy, barking without ceasing, running at the garden fences barking at passers-by. She would bark when the doorbell rang and run around the room jumping on all the furniture, knocking cushions off the settee, cups and plates onto the floor. She would often then run from room to room, up and down stairs barking. The barking was very shrill, and Jill had received several complaints from neighbours.

On walks Rosie pulled constantly, often walking and bouncing on her hind legs whenever she saw people and especially other dogs. Their daily walk took them past fields with cows and sheep, which she would persistently bark at too

In the garden, when not running along the fence barking, she would find places to dig or be so focused on an area that she would refuse to pay any attention to Jill.

Jill was most concerned about the barking in the house and garden owing to the complaints. Rosie would sometimes bark at night-time and take a long time to settle down.

Rosie was a very high energy dog, who was rarely still. She had occasionally nipped Jill when Jill picked her up in order to try to calm her down. Jill was also worried that Rosie may one day bite her grandchildren as she had sometimes taken the toys off them and refused to give them back. She would under these circumstances growl at the children.

It was explained that Rosie's stress bucket was very full and because she was so hyper-vigilant, she was experiencing negative emotions and stress. The calmness circle was discussed together with other calming games. It was explained that preventing Rosie rehearsing the unwanted behaviour was a key part of her training.

Crate games were demonstrated and practiced. It was easy to move the crate around the house since Rosie only needed a small, lightweight crate. Having Rosie being able to settle in the crate was fundamental to her relatively quick success at learning new behaviour.

Jill opted to place the covered crate in a back bedroom, drawing the curtains and playing soundtracks designed for dogs. Instrumental and classical music was also an option. This helped to mask external sounds that Rosie had previously reacted to by barking.

Most of Rosie's daily allowance of food was fed in the crate, in the form of puzzle toys, Kongs etc. Bones and chews were also given.

Calmness games were played in one room of the house. Rosie was prevented from running from room to room by tethering her to Jill (to a belt around the waist, so hands free). Doors were kept shut and baby gates utilised where most convenient.

After three days (to ensure an empty stress bucket) Jill took Rosie into the garden to play calmness games there. Games were kept under three minutes and then going back into the house. Jill chose the quietest times of day to go outside.

This strategy meant that the previous routine of going on walks was 'ditched' as were Rosie's mealtimes. Jill practised putting the harness on and taking it off again whenever she remembered as frequently as was convenient. She noticed that Rosie soon stopped going hysterical whenever she saw her leash and harness. Jill then started to play the calmness games when Rosie was wearing the harness and then taking it off again. Rosie started wearing the harness and just going in the crate to chew a Kong.

Jill was so committed to Rosie's rehab that she even disconnected the doorbell and put a note on the door to telephone. She organised for her friends and family to telephone before visiting so she could put Rosie in the back bedroom with a Kong and her music. Once her visitors were settled, Rosie would join them – on a leash initially to prevent her running round the room. Jill would give her treats or scatter feed some kibble on the floor.

Friends and family were very complimentary to Jill as to the improvements they saw within a week. Rosie met them without barking and very quickly settled in the room. Before visitors were ready to leave, Jill took Rosie back upstairs to the crate, gave another long-lasting chew, and quietly and calmly saw her visitors out.

Jill chose to drive Rosie to quiet locations to walk her. She focused on the games including ones for loose leash and recall. Rosie was kept on a long line on walks and in the garden, so she did not rehearse the behaviour of refusing to recall.

Within a week Jill saw huge improvements, Rosie settled quickly and slept so much more. Six weeks later, Rosie is much quieter, Jill can quickly interrupt any over excited behaviour and ask Rosie to go to her crate. Since their relationship has improved and Rosie has enjoyed playing the games with Jill she now recalls from the garden whenever Jill wants her to. Jill is careful only to have her out for short periods, so she does not fall into previous habits.

Jill monitors Rosie's interaction with her grandchildren, supervising any playing with toys that Rosie may want. She ensures Rosie is given her own toys and her grandchildren leave Rosie to play with her toys. Rosie only spends short periods with the children and is much calmer. As soon as Jill feels Rosie has had enough or her bucket is filling, she removes her for some quiet time. Rosie has not growled at the children since the strategies were put in place and is now much more relaxed with them.

Summary

- In this chapter we have looked at the personality traits of optimism, pessimism, the tolerance of frustration, flexibility, whether your dog is a thinker or a doer.
- We also discussed how knowing breed characteristics can be useful, but the most important thing is to train the dog in front of you.
- There are huge ranges of personalities and characteristics with a breed. Your dog's ability to learn will vary depending on the stress bucket threshold and his emotions on the day.

Mythbuster Moment: You cannot train dogs bred to hunt to recall off their chosen prey. For example: An Afghan Hound will not recall once it has caught sight of a running rabbit. Another example: You will never get your husky to recall away from prey.

If you work through the stages, following the information and playing the games you will be able to have a consistent recall. In the interest of safety, you may still choose to keep a long line on, or ensure you are in a secure field. Always work towards the best recall you can have. You never know when you may need it.

In the next chapter we will take a look at how we can shape the personality and create the behaviour we prefer.

GAMES TO SHAPE YOUR DOG'S PERSONALITY

CHAPTER INTRODUCTION:

Dealing with anxious, fearful and nervous dogs through optimism games. Tolerating frustration and helping flexibility.

Optimism:
- Cone/Harness shaping.
- Front Feet, Back Feet and All Feet.
- Novel Objects, noise box.

Tolerating Frustration:
- Treat dispensers, Kongs and scatter feeding.
- Race to toys or food.

Helping Flexibility:
- 'Try Something Different' Game
- Ditching the routine and adding variety to games.

A brief testimonial of Tiggy, a female Belgian Shepherd.

"I have had so much fun playing the optimism games with Tiggy, my Shepherd. At the start we did not seem to make much progress and I did not think she really enjoyed the games, but then after a telephone call, I realised that I had pushed forward too fast. Tiggy is timid and I was putting too much pressure on her. Worse, my feelings of frustration were not helping. I was reminded to give some easy wins and not always make it harder and harder.

I have discovered that I too lack flexibility and can be pessimistic. For me, making a list of games to play helped otherwise I kept playing the same ones for too long. I found it hard to change from the idea of a 30-minute training session to 24/7 training with a maximum of a three-minute gaming session. Tiggy is now a happy and much more confident dog, we are able to enjoy our walks together and our playing in the garden. I no longer feel stressed worrying about how she is going to react. She used to panic if anything was different in the house and try to hide away."

The pessimistic Tiggy will be inclined to be worried about ambiguous or strange/novel things. This negative emotion will be filling the stress bucket. This often results in the 'reactive' dog, the one that barks, spins, lunges etc. Often the small triggers are not picked up by the owner. Working with a pessimistic dog who has a constantly full stress bucket is next to impossible. Remember the full bucket is over threshold, this means Tiggy is incapable of learning or being thoughtful. When working on optimism we have an emptier bucket and are unlikely to go over threshold.

Games to Play for optimism and confidence

These help the nervous, anxious or reactive Tiggy. You can be very creative about the games you play. It is more about making it easy for Tiggy to be successful, for giving her easy wins so she feels positive associations.

Shaping

You may already be familiar with shaping behaviour, perhaps using a clicker. The essence is to break the final goal into small steps. If you want Tiggy to go into a crate or onto a boundary, you reward any movement towards the crate/boundary. Initially it may be just looking at it. Essentially, it's a problem-solving exercise, with a fun element of reward. Easy wins and no pressure. You may use a marker word, instead of a clicker, where you say 'yes' or something similar and then give her a treat. If you use a clicker or marker word, then you need to have previously associated it with the treat – e.g. say 'yes' and give a treat. Markers do help in that you can give instant reinforcement, even when the delivery of the treat may be slightly delayed.

Cone/harness shaping

You can choose anything to shape, it does not have to be useful. We have already discussed shaping to a harness, collar and leash. You can shape for Tiggy to put her nose into a cone. We're using the same principles as the 'Put your nose in it' game in chapter 2.4.

Front feet, back feet, all feet

The aim is for her to put her front feet onto an object, for example a chair, cushion or book. This is started at home (as always) where Tiggy is happy and calm. It can then be taken out into the environment once she is used to it. You can ask for front feet on objects such as benches or a low wall. Be creative.

It's a little harder to do a similar exercise with the back feet, maybe all four feet if the object is suitable. Tiggy is also learning flexibility with this. It may be the same object but you're asking for a different way of interacting with it. Do you want her front feet, back feet or all four feet?

Novel objects and noises.

Be inspirational and creative. Baby steps, build slowly, with no pressure. Ensure it is Tiggy's choice to interact with the novel, potentially scary object. Start in the safe environment knowing Tiggy has an empty bucket. Initially, it may simply be a box in the room. Think about scattering treats around the box, if the box is shallow place some treats in it. You can build up to Tiggy getting in the box. Later, place other objects in and around the box. Maybe eventually add some objects that make a slight noise when moved. Toss treats in the box amidst the objects. Remember to always go back a few stages and give easy wins periodically.

Tiggy is in charge. It is her choice and she is in control of whether she interacts or not. Be guided by her behaviour. You may need to make it easier. Keep all games short, three minutes is plenty. With a very anxious dog, maybe keep to thirty seconds.

Training is 24/7 so although you may only play a game for thirty seconds, you can choose to play a different game a few minutes later if you choose. Over the day you can have plenty of short inspirational, fun interactions. All adding to your relationship bank account.

Through this, Tiggy is gaining in confidence and having a more optimistic outlook, remaining in 'happy land'. As she becomes more optimistic in the house, you can move to the garden (if suitable) or any other place that you have control of and know Tiggy is calm and happy in. Place some novel objects in the garden. You could start with the same box, as it is often challenging enough that the box is now in a different place.

Always when you move to a new location, ensure her stress bucket is empty, that you both have a calm mindset and go back a few stages every so often. Best to make only one change at a time, unless you are very confident Tiggy can handle more than one.

Keep it easy, keep it fun, keep it no pressure, Tiggy's choice to interact with her being in control.

Games to build tolerance of frustration

Life is frustrating, training can be frustrating. Anticipated outcomes and events may not happen quickly enough for Tiggy, or even at all. A dog with a low tolerance of frustration can become very distressed. It is very valuable to improve the capacity for being able to tolerate frustration and keep the bucket empty.

Treat dispensers

In 2.2, when discussing calming activities mention was made of using Kongs and various puzzle toys. Further discussion of 'ditch the bowl' and the routine all link with building optimism and tolerance of frustration. Which strategies or games you play, together with the level of difficulty, will depend on Tiggy's personality: her optimism and tolerance of frustration. The presentation of a Kong filled with frozen kibble will not be a calming activity for a hugely pessimistic Tiggy with poor frustration tolerance. It is likely to add to the stress bucket. She may be nervous of this strange rubber thing (novel object) initially and incapable of working out how to access the kibble. She may be too anxious to eat. Start at a level and place that is perfect for Tiggy, where she is calm and happy so she is able to learn and develop her new personality.

If Tiggy seems to lose interest, and starts sniffing for example, with any of the games it may be an indication that she finds the frustration too high. Take that as valuable information and go back a few stages, check her energy level. Maybe use some calming activities. Check that she can think.

When first using treat dispensers such as Kongs, where food is placed inside start with easy wins. Small pieces of high value kibble or other suitable food which fall out readily as the Kong is investigated by Tiggy. For a very pessimistic Tiggy, maybe start with kibble sprinkled around the Kong. Progression is made to using a paste with kibble inside the Kong. This is harder for her and builds up the ability to deal with the frustration of having to work for the food. You can then start to pack the Kong a little more, so it becomes a little harder. Throw in some easy wins with tasty small pieces of cheese that fall out easily. As you make things harder, you may choose to increase the value of the food you are using. Eventually, you may progress to freezing the Kong – initially for half an hour. Later you may move on to an hour or more. You get the picture.

The games introduced in the Scent chapter (3.4) will also help to build tolerance of frustration and help with optimism. Hiding food and Tiggy finding it. This can also be done with valued toys. Tiggy can be restrained whilst you hide the toy or food, and then released. Again, building tolerance of frustration.

Scatter feeding

We discussed scatter feeding in chapter 2.2 where we said to 'ditch the routine'. Scatter feeding is perfect for calming and building a tolerance of frustration.

If Tiggy starts barking then she may be finding the activity too challenging, she could also be having fun and showing enthusiasm. You will be the judge of what is working for you both. You may decide to calm things down and make it easier for a while before raising the bar again. Keep throwing in the easy wins, set Tiggy up for success for optimism and positive experiences.

Given that you are involved in all these games, controlling the resources such as food and toys, being associated with great fun, you will also be boosting your relationship. However, if the level of frustration is too high, then you are triggering a negative emotion. Negative emotion plus high arousal will be likely to leash to fear, see the circle of emotion in 1.3.

I'll Race you

Set up a favourite toy or food so Tiggy can see it. Simply hold her gently, maybe with a hand in front of her chest (if appropriate), just a second or so initially, and then allow her to race to the toy or food. To make the game more fun, you can pretend to race to the toy or food yourself. You can progress to requesting other behaviour that Tiggy can do e.g. a sit and then release to the toy/food. It livens up the session, and boosts flexibility, if you change the toy and food reward frequently.

It is often easier for Tiggy to cope with frustration if she can keep moving. One game that builds tolerance but enables her to move is pole wrapping. Any object can be used: a bin, pole, chair, cone etc. Teach her to leave you, run around the object, and return for a treat. To teach this initially, the object can be very close to you, you can shape or lure around the object, and treat on return. Increase the distance gradually – remember to include some easy wins. You can increase the number of wraps, or send away again, thus delaying reward (building tolerance of frustration).

Training for Flexibility

As discussed in 3.1, if we want Tiggy to offer a new/different behaviour in a specific situation then she needs to be able to be flexible in her thinking. To learn to try out new behaviour and enjoy offering new behaviour. Instead of reacting by barking we want her to choose to check in and engage with you.

Any variation of the front feet game is valuable. Consider nose targeting various items. Or, with the same object teaching a paw touch. This may start out with the right front paw, but then rewarding a left front paw. How about trying a rear paw? Then the other rear paw? You can develop flexibility, and creativity by rewarding new interactions with the familiar object. This all helps build up Tiggy's flexibility and confidence.

The 'Try Something Different' Game

To create flexibility, creativity, motivation, and the ability to think through arousal or frustration productively, the 'Try Something Different' game is great for this. Reward anything, as long as Tiggy is not repeating a previously offered behaviour. This can be quite challenging, so best not done in the early weeks, when you are still promoting calm and safety. Practice games such as this to develop the concept of flexibility before trying this game. Keep it short and sweet, to avoid too much arousal and frustration. It can only be at the level Tiggy can cope, with and still think, and be motivated. You are gradually pushing the boundaries, but not too far or fast.

Any behaviour or movement your dog offers, tiny movements, and maybe any previously learned behaviours, such as paw/nose targeting, sit, lie down are all rewarded. The rule is that Tiggy is only rewarded once for each new behaviour, she needs to think of, and perform a different one (or sufficiently different) to obtain a reward. Watch out for Tiggy doing a repetitive chain of behaviour, she can catch you out.

It can be fun to play the 'Try Something Different' game using your body. After shaping/training Tiggy to be comfortable standing between your legs when you are standing and facing the same direction, see if she offers a sit, lie down, even moving forward or backwards with you. Leg weaves, where Tiggy threads between your legs as you slowly walk forward, raising your legs to allow her to pass using either leg or direction to start. Try using your body to wrap around, instead of a cone or pole etc. There is no limit to this game but remember to keep the frustration and arousal within Tiggy's ability to still think. Don't put too much pressure on her and always keep it fun with positive associations.

This is a good place to point out that frequent changes of the reward you offer such as different foods and toys build flexibility, they keep sessions fun and interesting.

<u>Games for a Thinker:</u> To help Tiggy become a more balanced dog, you can use games that encourage movement and transitions. You may consider teaching spins, lots of 'middle on the move', running to a target to place a paw or running around poles. In the next chapter there are many games requiring a little more arousal and movement. Whilst these are suggested as games for recall, loose leash walking etc, they will also help with becoming more of a Doer.

<u>Games for a Doer:</u> If you want Tiggy to become more thoughtful, to not rush in and offer even more speed, consider employing games that are about stillness and duration. For example, sit or lie down. Having Tiggy's focus more on precision rather than speed. Using platforms and foot targets are perfect for this. Tiggy can learn to have each paw on an object such as an over-turned bowl. You can work up to using four bowls on a suitable surface, building up to each paw on one bowl. Any game that requires precision will help to develop a Thinker.

A Brief Case Study

Tom arranged his and Tiggy's consultation as he was concerned that she was becoming very reactive on walks, especially towards other dogs and, as Tom noticed, anything that was strange, or that she had not seen before. This could sometimes be something she had seen before but was in a different location. He found Tiggy very unpredictable as sometimes she would seem ok with a dog ten metres away and other times, she would react to the same dog thirty metres away.

Tiggy was becoming more reactive (barking, pulling and lunging) towards traffic, especially bikes. She particularly seemed to find the act of little dogs being picked up by their owners something very hard to deal with calmly. Tiggy is a predominantly black, large dog so would seem very intimidating when she was barking loudly, showing her teeth and pulling forward. To most people she looked as if she wanted to attack. At home, Tiggy showed nervous behaviour when meeting Tom's friends and family, often trying to hide and run into another room.

Tom was given the link to online resources which had more games and information on ditch the routine, bowl, and a wealth of great games to play with Tiggy. He was advised to give Tiggy as much rest as possible and for a few days to remain at home.

It was decided that scent games would be very beneficial as calming activities and one way to boost Tiggy's confidence. The first stages in scent games were demonstrated and others described.

Tom was introduced to the games for optimisms: cone and harness shaping, front feet and all feet on and scatter feeding over and around novel objects and noise boxes. The games were demonstrated with care given Tiggy's anxiety level. High value treats were used. Initially a shallow cardboard box was used with a couple of regularly seen objects inside, such as egg cartons.

Games for flexibility and dealing with frustration were also chosen. Tom was instructed to play each game for just a few repetitions and carefully watch Tiggy's body language. Sonia highlighted how important it is to ensure that Tiggy remained relaxed and calm. We had several Skype coaching calls with Tom, as well as some telephone conversations to help keep on track.

Great progress was made within the first week, with Tiggy being much calmer at home. Then Tom reported that he felt she was not enjoying the games and was finding them stressful, choosing to lie down instead.

Tom took some videos of him playing with Tiggy and sent them to Sonia. Several changes were made, sessions were even shorter. Tom softened his body language and paid attention to his tone of voice, eye contact and position. Tom had had other dogs and was used to the idea of being the boss, giving commands and expecting compliance. To learn how to simply have fun, put no pressure on was difficult for him.

Eight weeks later, Tiggy was making huge progress. She was joyful playing the games, much more optimistic and enjoying working out the puzzles being set. She was a very intelligent dog who once the fear was removed, learnt very quickly, completely surprising Tom. From him judging her to be 'not very bright' he now thinks she is the most 'intelligent dog I have owned'. Their relationship has improved enormously and Tiggy is so much more confident and happy.

Summary

In this chapter we have described some games that will transform your relationship, building optimism, flexibility and the ability to tolerate frustration.

Optimism
- Cone/Harness shaping.
- Front Feet, Back Feet and All Feet.
- Novel Objects, noise box.

Tolerating Frustration:
- Treat dispensers, Kongs and scatter feeding.
- Race to toys or food.

Helping Flexibility:
- 'Try Something Different' Game
- Ditching the routine and adding variety to games.

Mythbuster Moment: My dog is not food motivated so I cannot play the games using food.

If you ditch the bowl and work on animating the food, you can create a food motivated dog who will love working for even a piece of kibble. Keep the pressure off and the games fun. Sessions short and sweet and ensure your dog is in a calm but interested emotional state. Take control of the environment and distractions.

The next chapter will dig deeper into other games that help with calmness and hugely enrich your dogs' life. We will be describing how to introduce your dog to scent games. Whatever your struggle, scent games will help you.

GAMES TO ACHIEVE LOOSE LEAD WALKING, RECALL AND IMPULSE CONTROL

CHAPTER INTRODUCTION:

Dealing with reactivity in dogs. Lessening lunging, barking and general aggression.

- 'Eyes on me' game
- 'Love my name'
- 'It's Raining Treats'
- 'Two leads'
- 'Leash off play and leash on play'
- 'Middle In Between'
- 'Catch me if you can'
- The opposite 'ball chucker' game
- 'Flirt pole'

A brief testimonial of Bertie, a male Basset Hound.

"It's such a simple idea to make yourself more interesting than the environment yet it's so powerful. I love having a dog that stays close to me, keeps checking in with me and has brilliant recall. The best thing about it is that we had so much fun learning and it all came together so quickly. Amazing."

Loose leash walking and recall games

One very common struggle is Bertie pulling on the leash, making walking him very difficult and frustrating. It may even mean only one person in the household has the strength to hold him.

Another common struggle is lack of reliable recall, this means Bertie needs to stay on the leash which is often, as given above, another struggle.

A rescue dog is likely not to have had great training and, of course, has not built up an awesome relationship with you yet. Often, you are working from scratch. Even harder, it may be that they believe pulling on the leash is the only way to get from A to B, as that is what they have done in the past. They may have learnt to ignore their name whilst on walks, especially if the environment is very exciting to them e.g. around other dogs, chasing a squirrel etc.

Imagine where your relationship will be so strong that you will trust Bertie and have confidence in him to always recall. Where you don't even need a leash to have him by your side, whenever you want. Where he actively wants to pay attention to you. The plan is to add so much value and fun that Bertie chooses to be with us with great manners in all places and habitats. This is achievable if you follow this integrative process of games, setting up for success, baby steps and shaping Bertie's personality.

<u>'Eyes on me'</u>: You want Bertie to always choose to look to you, to orient to you, to check out where you are rather than you frantically keeping eyes

on him. Think about how the young of a species needs to check out where mum is to keep safe.

The same principles apply as earlier games, baby steps, working at home, in the garden and then gradually more challenging environments with more distractions. Ensure Bertie is set up for success and follow the 95% rule.

Place food on the floor and wait for Bertie to eat it, when he has finished eating, he will look at you wondering if there is more to come. When he looks at you, say your marker word for example, 'yes' in a happy voice and feed another piece. You are simply encouraging Bertie looking/orienting to you.

You can extend this game by rolling some food away from you, allowing Bertie to chase and eat it then look back to you, say 'yes' and roll another piece of food. Repeat a few times.

Remember not to pressure him, keep it short and sweet without too many repetitions.

<u>'Love my Name':</u>Many rescue dogs have learned to ignore the calling of their name or even have negative associations with their name as they have been told off using their name many times. Often their name is shouted using an angry tone. We can choose to use another name or sound with no baggage attached or work with the original name extra hard.

If you know other people are going to be using Bertie's name in a negative way, with inconsistency, then we encourage you to have a special name or recall word. One that only you (or other trusted people) use. Our huskies work with many people who are always calling their names inappropriately, usually because they want a good photo with the husky and their family. Therefore, for recall, we have a completely different sound. We do find if we say their name, they do pay attention to us. But, it's good to have the extra word as backup.

Assuming you are using their name, you need to add so much value to the name by rewarding Bertie every-time you say it. Throw food out for

Bertie to chase and eat. From playing the previous game, you will know he is just about to turn and look at you, just before that moment say his name. When he turns and comes back to you reward him with a high value treat. Throw another lower value treat for him to chase, when he eats it say his name, as he turns and comes back to you, he can receive another great treat.

An improvement of this would be to make yourself very inviting as he looks to you. Say his name and move backwards in a lower position (almost like a version of a play bow). This will encourage Bertie into your space especially if he is generally more timid. You can practice this as a stand-alone game. Wait for him to look at you, say his name, walk backwards. Use a happy voice and smile, as he comes to you give a great treat. Don't fall into the mistake of repeating Bertie's name. Once is enough.

'Funnel': This builds great value in proximity to you. It's great fun and gives confidence. Above all, it encourages Bertie to run quickly towards you. He'll run through your legs, return and repeat. Many dogs stop just out of reach, maybe reaching with their nose to take a treat and then promptly reversing out of reach. They want the treat but do not want to go back on the leash. This game brings them quickly, with no pressure to where it is very easy for you to reach them.

Choose a piece of food that Bertie can easily see, consider the colour of the ground and the treat. Make sure there is a clear contrast so he can see it. You may need to lure Bertie through initially if he is low confidence. Let him follow a tasty treat through your legs from the front to behind you and then toss it a foot or so away. Bertie should chase the food, eat it and turn around, orienting back to you. Have a second piece ready, you may need to lure him again, throw and repeat. After a few turns Bertie should happily have the idea of running between your legs for the treat. He may still choose to go around you if not initially comfortable with going between your legs, so don't worry if you need to lure for a few more turns.

As confidence improves you will be able to throw the treat further, which gives you more time to turn around and throw another piece. Up to ten repetitions are plenty.

> *Note: Always stop a game before Bertie loses interest or feels any pressure. Keep him wanting more.*

'It's Raining Treats'

Teach Bertie to catch pieces of food by dropping a small, but easy to see piece in front of his nose. Face in the same direction with Bertie at your side in the heel position. In order to catch, he will need to focus upwards to the hand. As he gets better at catching, the game becomes more powerful. You will then be able to walk forwards; Bertie then focuses on your hand and catches the treats as you walk. The intense focus and fun can help enormously when passing previously challenging hazards. Remember to practice at home, hone the skill then go out and about. Short and sweet. Keep it fun and happy. This way, Bertie becomes so in tune with you, and looks to you rather than the hazard. This could be anything from an off-leash dog to a cat.

'Two leash game': Often the sound of the leash unclipping is the trigger for Bertie to run off with great excitement. This is not what we generally want. Hopefully, the games you have played previously at home such as putting harness, collars, leads off and on unpredictably so as not to trigger excitement, will still work outside. If not, then work with this game. Have two leads, unclip one but keep the other on so Bertie cannot run off. As you unclip one leash give Bertie some food with your other hand immediately, then clip the leash back on. Thus, unclipping the leash is associated with staying for food, not immediately running off. You have managed the situation by preventing the previously learned behaviour of running off immediately from happening. This helps Bertie to remain calm when the leash unclips. A calm dog chooses great behaviour, orienting to you, maybe waiting for great games to start instead of zooming off.

'Leash off play and leash on play': Unclip your leash (you can still have a long line on if needed) then play Bertie's favourite games. This way, he prefers to stay and have fun with you rather than run off. As usual, this can be practiced in less challenging environments initially. Also, upon recalling and putting the leash back on, play another exciting game. Recall him, then give a treat and play a game without putting the leash on. With this method, whether the leash is on or off, you are fun to be with. Mix it up. The leash is never punishing, it is not associated with fun is over now.

'Middle In Between': This game builds value, teaches proximity without pressure and adds a safe place for Bertie. Lure Bertie between your legs with him facing in the same direction as you, give a little bit of backwards pressure on Bertie's chest, his reflex will be to push back and move forward.

You can lure Bertie from either side into middle position between your legs and release with food thrown forward. Make sure you use your chosen release cue. As always set up for success. Make it easy and obvious at the beginning, maybe with luring and saying the middle cue when you know Bertie will be following the lure anyway. Soon, wherever Bertie is, when you say middle he will run between your legs. He may do this by running backwards if he is in front of you when you say middle. Bertie may choose the quickest, most efficient way of getting to middle and having his treat. This is an awesome recall game with a cue that has not been previously 'poisoned' as previous recall cues may have been due to prior attempts at teaching them. This is often the case with Rescues. It is very easy to put the leash on in the middle position, whilst giving treats. Practice taking the leash off and on in this position.

'Catch me if you can': You may have noticed that Bertie loves to chase. How about he chases you instead of the bunny? With him off leash, choose an obstacle for example, a tree. Wait for him to orient to you, run quickly around the tree, this may be a yard or so away. Bertie will catch you quickly. When he does, have a party with lots of reward and fun for him. You can add your recall cue, run off round the tree and reward him when you're caught. You can increase the distance and Bertie's drive by having someone gently restrain Bertie and then release.

The opposite 'ball chucker' game: Instead of building value away from us by throwing the ball with the chucker, put some food in it and hold it just above Bertie's head for upward focus. As Bertie looks at it, drop it down for him to eat the treat. Repeat a couple of times then try walking with the chucker, Bertie will keep the upward focus and stay near you. This helps in building value in proximity once again.

'Flirt Pole': The Flirt Pole game is great for tolerance of frustration; this can help with arousal up and arousal down. It is an awesome game to play for extra focus and for us to be more fun than the environment. Thus, keeping Bertie engaged with us, not the distraction.

The above are only a few of many games that you can play to build value in proximity to you. The aim being that Bertie chooses not to pull on the leash and has a brilliant recall.

Remember, keep all games short and sweet. Use the 95% rule. You can change games frequently, be creative, fun and never pressure your pooch. Be aware of needing to raise the value of the food if you are going to a more challenging environment. Keep any changes as baby steps. If Bertie's stress bucket is fairly full, it is best not to raise the challenge that day, instead go for the easy wins.

A Brief Case Study

Bertie had no leash manners, pulling so hard that only Collin was able to walk him. He had zero recall and had to be on the leash at all times. He generally ignored commands given to him such as coming in from the garden, or even when being called by Ann or Collin in the house. He was described as being very stubborn. He often raided the bins; he would steal food off plates and out of Ann's hands. He was generally a relaxed, calm and confident dog.

The focus for Bertie was to play games designed to boost the relationship, improve loose leash walking and recall. Bertie being food motivated made this process easy. His daily allowance was used in playing the games. Games were initially kept very short, with frequent changes and rest periods. The aim was for Bertie to find joy in interacting with Colin and Ann and ignoring distractions.

Scent games were very valuable for boosting the relationship. Once Bertie realised that he had access to all sorts of interesting scents and tasty food on cue from Colin or Ann he soon started to pay attention to them.

Bertie will walk calmly on a loose leash when requested. Ann uses a walking belt and long leash if she wants to take him and allow him to enjoy the environment. She is confident to take him on walks knowing that she can request him to walk alongside her without pulling.

His recall has improved enormously; he consistently recalls at home, in the garden and low distraction environments. If he gets the scent of something very interesting that can still lead him to disengage, he is put on a long line. This means if he is recalled he is unable to practice the unwanted behaviour of ignoring the cue and carry on following the scent.

Collin and Ann agree that they have a much-improved relationship with Bertie, they enjoy that he initiates playing the games and comes to them for attention now.

Summary

In this chapter we have introduced several quick and fun games to boost the relationship. These will give real life results, awesome recall and loose leash walking.

Loose leash walking and recall games

- 'Eyes on me' game
- 'Love my name'
- 'It's Raining Treats'
- 'Two leads'
- 'Leash off play and leash on play'
- 'Middle In Between'
- 'Catch me if you can'
- The opposite 'ball chucker' game
- 'Flirt pole'

Mythbuster Moment: I do not have the time to train my dog.

The games are as short at ten seconds up to a maximum of three minutes. In three minutes, you can play up to ten games – thirty seconds each. Even ten short sessions choosing one game may only take ten minutes. Games can be played walking from room to room, when the kettle is boiling, waiting for the microwave to ping. Easy, quick, simple and fun.

In the next chapter we will introduce scent games, whatever your struggle these games will help you.

GAMES TO SKYROCKET YOUR PARTNERSHIP

CHAPTER INTRODUCTION:

Scent Games and Puzzle Toys; Scent is a powerful motivator and is generally a calming activity. Monitor the body language and be aware of your dog's excitement level. If it's too high, you may reduce the value of the food rewards.

- 41% of your dogs' brain is used for smell.
- Training for specific scents.
- Boundaries in scent games.
- Switching from anxious to calm.
- Stop fixation and stalking.
- Build confidence and focus to help ignore distractions.
- Provide enrichment that ticks your dogs need to engage with their nose.

A brief testimonial of Sam, a male Labrador.

"I have adored teaching Sam scent work. It has transformed our time together. Clearly, he needed to do this. I worried that, in doing this work, it would make it worse when we went out on walks. He loves to smell things. Instead, because he has so much opportunity and fun when we do the games together, he is not bothering so much when on walks. I can now always call him away if I wish to. I found giving a 'go sniff' command and then letting him sniff meant I was able to call him back to me with more fantastic games. His recall is now pretty perfect, it used to be that if, he was distracted, I had no recall. It is lovely to give him more freedom now knowing he listens to me."

Around 41% of Sam's brain is dedicated to scenting. Clearly, this is important to him. He explores by sniffing; he communicates and interacts with his world this way. Originally for dogs it was vital to safety and survival.

The benefits of scent work are huge. It is very usual that Sam will choose to sniff something interesting rather than listen to you. Scent is a powerful motivator for Sam. We can use this motivation to work with it as a reward rather than setting ourselves against it. Throughout this book this principle has been expounded. Work with Sam's drives, not against them.

Scent work is perfect for low confidence dogs, the previous concerns fade as they focus on the scent. It builds optimism, confidence, trust, connection and the brilliant relationship you want. It can even help with impulse control. It is something you and Sam can do together whilst ensuring the stress bucket empties. Because it is a brain activity and calming, after the game Sam will be happy to rest and sleep. Sam can concentrate his energy on building focus, the ability to tolerate frustration, and being able to think in arousal. All the things that will help Sam become happy and secure in our human world. Please make scent work part of yours and Sam's life together.

One of the activities you will probably have encouraged on the boundaries or crate is to lie down. You may have even put it on a cue. This will be the way your dog will let you know when he has found the scent focus. So really practice Sam's lie down cue. It is easy to see from a distance. You can choose to use any behaviour and put it on cue for Sam's signal to you that he has found the scent. For the sake of this example, assume you have chosen a lie down position

You can power up your lie down cue before beginning scent work. Remember to reward the steps Sam goes through to get a down. Re-teach the down. Give rewards as Sam starts to do steps towards a down, in the same way you taught the down initially. Then feed the ground between Sam's front legs when down. Give several pieces of food to the floor to encourage duration in the down and then give your release cue.

You will have already built confidence with the harness and leash. You can choose to use a specific harness for your scenting work. This helps Sam to know what the job is. Ensure Sam is comfortable with the harness before you work. It is best to use the back clip for scent work; the front clip is best to be associated with proximity and loose leash walking. The back clip means they are encouraged to give more distance and allowed to pull. With our huskies, the sledding harness means allowed and encouraged to pull. Whereas putting a leash on the collar and clear intention means closer, heel type work with no pulling.

Some dogs may need help to be happy with feeling pressure on the harness and still carrying on with task without backing off. Initially you can have Sam free especially if working at home in safe location. Using a leash attached to the collar can break their concentration. You can put the harness on and play a short fun game to raise the energy a little. Remember, we are building impulse control so first we do need the impulse namely the energy and drive to perform an activity. Train the dog in front of you.

To manage scents, you'll want something akin to a scent kit. This could be something like sweet birch, an essential oil in an airtight box. Then you can drill holes in the box, adding the filter tips. Just a couple of drops of oil are on the filter tips. You can re-use this in the next sessions or dispose as you need.

A good idea is to add magnets inside the container, so it sticks to metal surfaces for your convenience. Tweezers are useful for handling the filters to avoid handling and putting on human scent. You can prepare more filters and keep them in an airtight container to use another time. Be aware of Sam's sensitivity to the scent – it may be too much for them so use less oil.

If you present the scent when you are in front of the dog, it will be natural for Sam to investigate. With a nervous dog simply reward any forward movement. If Sam is not interested, then do not move it towards him. Feed him away from the container so it allows for resetting and re-seeking. Be natural and add no pressure. You don't need to repeat this much, perhaps use somewhere between five and ten repetitions. With a very shy low confidence dog, just do two or three. Ensure, when holding the container, you allow the air to flow through. Reward approaches initially, you can switch hands to keep interest and thinking. The container in one hand and reward in the other. This is about finding the scent, not just going to a particular hand or side. Keep it unpredictable. Sam has to locate the scent and find it.

You have plenty of options for what scent you wish to work with. Though check that it is safe for dogs. Often essential oils are used. Just a drop or two onto a little cotton wool/bud/filter is needed. It is best to use an oil that is not used in the house. Keep it unique. Reward is given to any movement towards the scent. You are encouraging Sam to sniff the container directly. You can use other scents simply follow the same process of rewarding the approach and interaction with the scent. Then you can simply swap hands and re-present the container.

Each time Sam sniffs the hand with the container he is praised or treated. You can then start to place the container in easy to find places and release your dog to find it. As with all the games, set up for success. Keep it easy and the games very short.

You can gradually build duration in that when Sam finds the container, he needs to stay with it and wait for you to arrive, praise and treat.

Once you have come this far you can choose the behaviour you want Sam to do when he finds the scent, so you know he has found it. This is likely to be a lie down as suggested earlier. This behaviour needs to be on cue, so you can give the cue e.g. 'down' when Sam finds the scent and lots of great reward.

Present the tin, let him sniff and cue 'down'. When he goes down reward him generously. You are establishing that when he locates the scent, he should lie down. The love and enthusiasm for the scent is increasing together with the confidence with such a fun and easy game. The old cue is the 'down' signal, the new cue is the scent. You will always present the new cue such as 'scent' just before the old cue 'down'. You can place the treat on the container. Remember to give the release cue from the down and reset.

It is best not to be in a hurry to put the down cue in to the game. Work on the scent drive desire and ensure Sam understands that he must find the scent first. Otherwise, he will possibly offer a down instead of finding the scent.

Now you are ready to take it further.

To increase desire, you can gently hold Sam as you place the scent slightly out of reach. This builds the drive. Once you release Sam, as his nose touches the container, cue 'down' and give rewards on the container itself. Also, if Sam watches you place the container, it builds up the drive and the fun.

When playing scent games outside, ensure you are playing into the wind. This way the wind blows the scent to the Sam. When Sam checks out other areas, do not to interfere, just allow Sam to work independently with no clues or the repeating saying of 'find it'. This will increase Sam's confidence. Sam does not go from A to B, he will sniff all around. As always, keep it easy and set up for success. If Sam does not find the scent, simply reset, perhaps going back a stage or two. You may have just been a little too enthusiastic yourself and moved forward a little too quickly.

You can then start to place the container just out of sight but allow Sam to watch the general area you have placed the container. Then release him to find. Once found, praise and reward. You can use a boundary to keep Sam in place as you do this if his boundary game duration and tolerance of distraction is sound enough. If you are still working on that and do not want to ask too much at this stage, you can use a long line and wrap it round a post or similar and then release.

Use baby steps, as always. Increase the distance slowly, maybe Sam does not know where to start looking, so needs to rely on the nose. This will build confidence and focus. Remember to give some easy wins, don't make it harder and harder. That adds pressure and can take away the fun and enthusiasm.

You can incorporate boundary game duration to help with scent work duration. Increase duration with boundaries separately, this will help Sam to build duration, waiting in a down position when finding the scent until his partner reaches him with the reward. Simply reward the boundary whilst Sam is on the boundary, remember calmness is important, it is not important what position Sam is in. He does not need to lie down, or sit, he just has to remain on the boundary. Remember to relax yourself if you wish Sam to relax.

Don't be rushed, as soon as you have marked the good choice you have plenty of time to give the reward. Slower placement of reward is beneficial for a more thoughtful, calm mindset, which is great for learning.

What about a Scent Distraction Action game?

Try gradually to have more distractions whilst Sam is on the boundary. This could be you stepping over him or someone walking past. Practice with the boundary first then, move on to the scenting scenario. Then we can apply the same level of distraction when Sam is in lie down position over the scent.

> Note: Train for the situation not when in the situation. We want Sam prepared to face it before it actually happens.

Once he's comfortable, you can start to have a slightly more complex environment with more places to hide the container. It can be fun to pretend to place the container somewhere that Sam sees you, but in fact you place it elsewhere. This increases the focus on the scent itself, not the sight of the container. It is a good idea for Sam to be able to transition from eyes to nose. Often, they can be a bit frantic when eye stalking.

Using the nose is utilising a more thoughtful part of the brain. This can help transition from 'scary land' to 'happy land'. From defensive vigilance to relaxing sniffing, then eating. Sniffing can be a transition activity to set Sam up to be able to take food as a reward. Remember the time when you could wave a top treat about and Sam completely ignored you. These games are key to the transition to having Sam's attention on your partnership.

You can use something, e.g. cushion, to hide the container to grow the game from in sight to out of sight.

Scent games have so many advantages.

They can be played indoors, in your garden and as with all other games start to take them to more distracting environments. Always keep to the 95% rule carefully monitor Sam's arousal level, his body language, set up for success. You want the value in the game to outweigh the challenge of a distracting environment.

Scent can help switch Sam from fear to calm and being able to think. It is probably the best way of all to communicate with your Sam, especially if he is a nervous guy who you are finding difficult to bond with. Scent games work with all breeds of dogs, even sight hounds: they simply choose sight first then nose. Some breeds are designed for scent work. They adore the activity. For a shy dog, once he loves the activity he can stop worrying about the environment. Scent work gives him something to do. It is mentally challenging and tiring. You do need to have frequent breaks to give the nose a rest too.

Many people may worry that it makes the dogs worse for sniffing, perhaps this is one of your struggles. Perhaps they sniff too much and ignore you? In reality, we are channelling the drive in a good way. Sam will not increase how much he sniffs when on a walk. It will become more efficient and appropriate, even better, on cue when you want. This way his sniffing can be turned on and off.

Scent games can help tick the box for the need and satisfy the drive. This is preferable to preventing Sam doing something he adores, withdrawing from your relationship bank account. Instead it enhances your relationship when you promote it and put it on cue. A brilliant teamwork activity to power boost your perfect partnership.

Scent games and puzzle toys.

You can use food and place it within puzzle toys. The scent of the food encourages Sam to solve the puzzle. This will also be a calming activity; using his nose, his brain and then chewing the food. There are a huge number of toys available for purchase, but you can also make your own. As many games as you can think of, the only limit is your creativity. A big part of the fun is thinking of new games.

A bottle that you have punched holes in and placed some kibble inside. As the bottle rolls kibble will spill out. A baking tray can have kibble placed within. The same with egg cartons. You can use a towel and roll up some food treats inside. Sam learns to unroll the towel to reach the treats.

Scatter feeding outside on the grass means Sam locates the treats by scent primarily. This game can be extended by hiding other treats/chews etc. Hiding them means Sam needs to use his nose not eyes. We find it is best to let Sam know when games start and finish. This will help avoid obsessive style searching when you have not put food out. You can give a release cue, e.g. 'get it' or 'find it', and then transition to another game to bring his focus back to you, perhaps "It's Raining Treats", then a boundary game. 'Nothing is Perfect' is hugely valuable.

You can hide treats under a cup for Sam to find. You can teach this game as a scent game. Let Sam see you place the treat under the cup and when he touches the cup with his nose, give him the treat. Then hide a treat under one cup but nothing under a second or even third cup. Sam needs to choose the correct cup. You can choose to extend this game by training the down when Sam is in front of the correct cup. Difficulty can be increased by having cups placed around the room and Sam needs to locate the cup with the treat and indicate by a down. 41% of your dogs' brain is used for smell.

A Brief Case Study

Philip brought Sam for a consultation as he wanted to improve his loose leash walking and recall. He has owned Sam for two years having adopted him from a rescue at six years old. Sam is a friendly, confident dog. Philip has been unable to have him off leash (unless in a secure, fenced area) and finds walking Sam quite hard work as he pulls constantly. He was using a choke collar to help control Sam. Sam will simply ignore Philip when on a scent trail or if he sees other dogs he wants to meet. He is a friendly dog both with people and other dogs.

Philip expressed concern on the initial telephone call that at eight years old it was too late to teach Sam to walk to heel and recall. He was reassured that we can teach old dogs new tricks.

During the consultation we discussed games to improve the relationship and thereby loose leash walking and recall. Sam was highly motivated by food which is always a bonus. He also adored scent work.

Sam's favourite games were eyes on me, 'It's Raining Treats', middle in between and the flirt pole using a ball attached to the line. These games built the positive relationship, wanting to be in proximity and the ability to listen even when excited.

Sam adored the scent work games; these games really boosted the partnership. Being able to put following a scent and searching on cue really helped. Sam is now very attentive to Philip, *waiting for the cue to 'go sniff' and will recall off, readily trusting that he will be playing yet more games very soon.*

Sam and Philip have now attended several scent workshops and some novice competitions with great success. Philip trusts Sam off leash and has integrated other games into their training together, so now can also request and receive loose leash walking.

Philip was so impressed by the effectiveness of the games he helps at dog training classes, demonstrating the games.

Summary

In this chapter we have described:

- Training for specific scents.
- Boundaries in scent games.
- Switching from anxious to calm.
- Stop fixation and stalking.
- Build confidence and focus to help ignore distractions.
- Provide enrichment that ticks your dog's need to engage with their nose.

Mythbuster Moment: my dog is not bred to follow scent so scent games will not work. He is bred to be a sight hound.

All dogs love to explore the environment using their nose. Some will take to scent games more readily and be easier to train up to the more difficult levels, but any dog will enjoy the more basic levels. Scent games will boost your partnership whatever the personality and breed of dog.

In this section of the book we have been looking at building an incredible partnership, boosting your relationship bank account by playing games. We have learnt how to select the games to suit the personality of our dogs and for how they are feeling that day. We have learnt about the value of calmness – never underestimate the importance of calmness. All the be-haviours you do want to come out of the calmness box.

So far in this book we have discussed the dog end of the leash, manage-ment of the environment to help set the scene for success and how to build the best partnership. In the next section we will look at the human end of the leash. Arguably the most important part – saved until last.

PART 4

THE HUMAN END
OF THE LEASH

4.1

CLEAR COMMUNICATION, LEADERSHIP AND ROLE MODELLING.

CHAPTER INTRODUCTION:

Clear communication is incredibly important in developing the partnership between you and your canine partner.

- Establishing a common language.
- Have you inadvertently taught your dog to ignore you?
- The mirror effect.
- Developing awareness for precision in your communication.
- Congruency.
- Patience.
- Interactive dialogue loop.
- Being present – your position and posture.
- Intention.
- Positive leadership.
- Clarity.

A brief testimonial of Roxy, a female Retriever.

"I loved learning about doggy body language and the importance of our communication being clear and consistent. I realised pretty quickly that I had been sending very confused and mixed signals. I can't believe how quickly Roxy started to listen to me once I ensured I was clear in my own mind. I needed to realise exactly what I wanted and pay attention to her responses to change my own. I learned to reframe from, 'what don't I want?' to 'what do I want?'. We are having so much fun, I was getting so frustrated and I am sure she was too. Having got that sorted out we are rocketing through the games and having fantastic results."

This chapter is all about developing an even more awesome partnership with Roxy. Clear communication is vital for a great partnership. We have discussed earlier about how it will be a work-in-progress. Learning Roxy's body language and how to pay attention to the whole context of the behaviour is vitally important to the relationship with her.

We are going to progress into an interactive dialogue, paying attention to the whispers and trying not to let the communication reach shouting stage (by either partner). Remember the stages from maybe a lip-lick to a bite? What about when the human partner becomes anxious, or frustrated, and shouts? Maybe even physically punishes Roxy, possibly feeling guilty afterwards? Either one of these scenarios will be withdrawals from the relationship bank account, damaging the trust and respect we are trying to build.

So how can we establish a common language, so you and Roxy find it easy to engage? A definition of Communication is 'the successful exchange of information, ideas and feelings.' Think about times we may have inadvertently taught Roxy to ignore us? This may be:

- When we ask for something that she is not able to do.
- When we are distracted, incongruent, or unsure.

- When we do not understand that we are maybe putting too much pressure on, not reading her communication accurately, and altering our behaviour accordingly.
- We expect Roxy to understand us and what we want, but often we do not take the trouble to understand Roxy and what she wants or needs.

Remember communication is two-way. We need to consider the following:

The senses: sight, hearing, touch, smell etc. Roxy's sense of smell is often her preferred way of gaining information about the world. The human prefers sight and hearing. How the human senses the world will be very different to Roxy's experience.

We want Roxy to keep us in her sight and we use our sounds (voice commands, whistle etc) to have a specific desired result. Always be aware of tone of voice, frequency etc. Soothing low, slow commands for calming her and high pitched, quick repetitive sounds for action. We want to use a 'happy voice' and smile when we want Roxy to recall.

Movement: Roxy is very sensitive to movement, more so than we are likely to be. Roxy is closer to nature than we are likely to be and is more tuned into the environment. Remember that she was originally a scavenger and predator, she is wired to chase after movement. We can use that. If we run, she will be wired to chase. This is generally a favoured game.

Emotions: Recall how this drives behaviour. Pay attention to Roxy's expression of her emotions. Gather feedback from her eyes, ears, mouth, posture, tongue, tail carriage and movement.

Intention: What is Roxy's idea behind her expression and action?

The mirror effect: Roxy will often mirror back to us what we have sent out to her. Anxious human can lead to anxious Roxy. A frustrated human can result in a fearful, frustrated Roxy. Maybe Roxy is shouting (barking) and human is also shouting. We can mirror our dogs too. On a positive note, a calm human will be mirrored by a calm Roxy.

Circle of understanding and cooperation

Consider that Roxy is gathering information about us too. She is likely to be more accurate regarding you than you are at reading her, especially as you are learning. The more awareness you have, the more precise your communication will be. Think back to calming signals and how, when we yawn, Roxy may mirror that with a yawn too. Perhaps when we lie down, Roxy will lie down.

Congruency:

Roxy knows how you really feel. You may be able to control your body language and facial expression to lie to a human, but Roxy will know it is not real. If you try for fake calmness, she will know. In fact, this can be more upsetting for her than when you are exhibiting anxious thoughts, anxious body language and speech. If you have anxious thoughts and emotions; but are trying to cover with relaxed body language and speech, it can be confusing for Roxy. Just as we want Roxy to be truly comfortable, calm and confident, we need to work on ourselves to be comfortable, calm and confident.

It is easier to change Roxy than ourselves. We like to point out that we seem to think Roxy needs to change and have more self-control etc, but what about the human's self-control? We need to work on mastering our thoughts, emotions and behaviour too.

Patience:

If we can be patient whilst Roxy processes the information, give her time and take the pressure off, it will lead to a more successful outcome. Often, we just need to wait for her to make the good choice and then really let her know we are happy with that choice.

The Interactive dialogue loop:

All communication/games/lessons will require you to be flexible. Remember to train the dog in front of you. You need to be clear of your goal. If you are stressed or distracted then remember the mirror effect, Roxy will be stressed and distracted too. Pay attention to Roxy's feedback.

Be present, live in the moment. If you are thinking of the future and what may happen, you may get anxious. If you are remembering the past, you may carry negative emotions from what happened then. Stay in the moment and remain focused with Roxy. You will need to be aware of the environment, but your main focus is Roxy. Being focused and present while we interact with Roxy is a learned skill that requires commitment and practice. Take it one moment at a time and build from there. It becomes easier with practice.

Think of having a bubble around you and Roxy. Keep the focus within the bubble. You can become so focussed that you don't even hear or see others around you. Make sure you are in a safe place when you are inside your bubble!

Position:

Where your body is facing and where your eyes are looking are hugely important. This is demonstrated very readily. You are either saying come close or move away. Our work with horses has shown us that, being a prey animal, they are very aware of eyes and the position of the predator. A sensitive horse is unlikely to load into a horsebox if the handler makes the mistake of looking back at her. Instead of moving forward up the ramp she is likely to run backwards. It looks like magic when someone else takes the leash-rope, looking to where they want to go, and the horse simply walks in. One seemingly small change with huge results.

We have worked with sensitive huskies who, for the first time, are pulling a rig. We've had plenty of examples where their owner/handler was alongside them encouraging them forwards with their voice but made the mistake of looking directly into her face. In this situation, the husky freezes and refuses to move forward. Once their owner looked forwards, the pressure was off, and the husky moved forwards.

You are often best to look where you intend to go, not at the hazard you want to avoid or have Roxy ignore. It's best that you ignore the hazard and focus on what you do want. Your orientation and where your eyes are facing are a big part of your communication. Roxy is likely to be paying attention to it. As your partnership improves so will her attention to your communication.

If you believe Roxy is trying to draw your attention to the hazard, you could briefly look at it and communicate it is no concern of yours or Roxy's.

Posture:

Your posture is either inviting, neutral, or repelling. A 'soft', low body is inviting, which is why a nervous Roxy is more likely to approach someone lying down or sitting on the floor. A genuinely smiling face and a happy voice is inviting. A standing tall, more arrogant type of stance with a stern, frowning expression repels or intimidates. No surprise there. Neutral is of course just that.

A lifetime working with horses, starting youngsters, and retraining 'problem' horses has been a great help to working with dogs. It is often more obvious if a horse is anxious and, of course, it is very important the signs are attended to otherwise we are likely to get hurt. Their feedback is instant.

We use our posture and position all the time working horses, it is amazing how much action we have from very subtle position changes. There is not the same tradition of using our voice as an aid or command. In some equestrian disciplines using the voice is frowned upon.

Think back to the recall games and when it was suggested you back away slightly with a soft, low, inviting posture to encourage Roxy to approach. Think about, in the absence of further training, that if you then step forward say to grab the collar Roxy is likely to move away. As you walk backwards, Roxy goes forwards and vice versa.

The above is natural communication between and within species, it can of course, be overridden with training or additional communication signalling you wish for a different response.

Your intention is powerful too. Again, this can be clearly demonstrated with horses. If you send a rope out towards a horse with the intention of desensitising her to a rope, she will remain standing. If you send it out to her in a similar manner and want her to move away, she is likely to do so. To the observer it may look the same action by the human, the horse will have picked up a shift in intensity and intention. Therefore, just as you need to observe Roxy's intention and intensity, she is reading yours. Be clear in your own mind what you intend to happen, visualise it.

Clear, consistent, and congruent communication is so valuable. Keep working on it.

How can I get Roxy's attention?

Get closer to Roxy, maybe even touch her in an inviting, playful way. Move away from Roxy in a fun and inviting, playful way. You can also make fun, high pitched, fast sounds. The 'happy' (maybe seen as silly) voice we use with young children works well for Roxy too.

Positive leadership:

Dogs thrive when they have clear guidelines. The more clarity you have, the easier and happier life gets for you and Roxy. Without that life can be confusing, difficult and frustrating.

Think of being a good parent, one who makes great decisions and helps to project security and safety. Role model appropriate behaviour. Be calm and confident. The parent is the great resource provider and keeps us safe and happy.

We may want Roxy to be happy and allow her access to great resources whenever she wants them. We like to let her choose. We may want to avoid any interaction which seems aversive or punishing in any way. In other words, being a permissive parent. But, sadly, Roxy is not likely to make great choices until she knows better.

Imagine the toddler who chooses all the e-number sweets, drinks, chocolate etc and decides he does not want his nap. Does what he wants to in company of others, at the table. He knows no rules of how to play nice. He is likely to be overstimulated and fractious. He is in no position to learn anything. His behaviour will likely get harder to deal with as he gets older. He does not sleep properly at night, is demanding, is stressed and likely to be neurotic and anxious. Such permissive parents however much they may love their child and want to make him happy are not doing him any favours by this leadership style. Think about that for Roxy.

Yes, we want a great partnership, but the human world is a challenging place for Roxy. Her instincts and drives are not best adapted to it without clear rules and boundaries. We need to show compassionate, intelligent leadership. We, personally, tend to hesitate before saying the word leadership in case it conjures up images of 'alpha dominance' ideas. We do not mean it in such a way. See chapter 4.2 for a discussion of this approach.

As you seek balance, you and Roxy will be more relaxed and connected. Having a purpose provides clear intentions and that leads to a collaborative partnership. Having a common purpose where Roxy and you want the same thing leads to Roxy being eager to collaborate. If we can shift our perspective to find a common purpose (e.g. safe, happy walks, playing fun games together, relaxing together) then Roxy will trust us more. We can enjoy fun experiments in solution seeking to replace the previous learning struggle.

Clarity questions:

What do you want Roxy to do? What do I want? Rather than what don't I want?

Why do I want Roxy to do it? How important is it to me?

What can I do to maximise success? What baby steps can I take to work towards the end goal?

How can I continue to gain Roxy's trust and help her gain confidence, for us both to feel safe, calm and happy?

We often, when doing a consultation, have people say to us, 'I just want to have a normal life with Roxy. I want to go on normal walks, to have a normal household where we can have people visit'. Frequently, we are asked how long it will take to turn Roxy into a normal dog.

Our answer would be, 'what is the definition of normal?' This is not easy to pinpoint. 'Normal' is simply a human construct. It turns out that few people have what they may think of as normal. Many people do struggle with stressful households. They may have 'difficult' dogs who become over excited when visitors arrive, struggles with loose leash walking and recall and so on. Think, instead, about what you would like to achieve. Why you want to achieve it? Consider what you need to do to reach the end goal. Is that end goal necessary for you and Roxy to be safe, calm and happy?

'How long will it take?'

'I cannot live like this for much longer, Roxy will need to be rehomed. She is causing arguments. She has done so much damage.'

'If it takes too long, I may need to re-home Roxy.'

Well, once again time is a human construct. Roxy is living in the moment and not worrying about next week. She is not worrying about last week either. If she is safe, calm and happy now. Well, that is perfect. Can we work at living in this moment, right now?

What can we do to remain safe, calm and happy? Just now, just today? If we are working with Roxy with the mindset that we may need to rehome her if things don't improve by a specific deadline then we are working with a negative mindset and putting pressure on the relationship. We're interacting with anxiety. We are not giving her a chance to feel secure with us, to feel loved. Please work towards simply going moment by moment, day by day.

You can set some goals and create a chart of small baby steps of how to achieve the goal. Though, this approach only works if it is how you like to plan anyway, but in using this method, you can clearly measure your progress which is motivating for you. We do recommend that you do this. Measuring your progress is hugely motivating.

To set yourself and Roxy up for success, remember to be focused and present, to pay attention to her communication with you, to be clear and consistent in your communication. Be prepared to change your training according to her feedback. You will be surprised at how quickly the relationship improves and Roxy is happy to make the choices you want her to make. Roxy's behaviour will change to what you do want surprising quickly.

If we are worried about having visitors, maybe family visiting. How creative can we be to keep Roxy safe, calm and happy, maybe in another room. Perhaps, going to stay for a few hours with a familiar person? If she is calmer in the car, (weather permitting) just chilling out. Does everybody have to meet her? If so, maybe just a short meet when everybody is calm, and you have had time to request how you would like them and Roxy to meet each other.

Yes, it may be Roxy's home and she is part of your family, but what would she prefer? Often our children would prefer to play happily and quietly up in their room, yet we insist they come and join the family. It goes on too long and ends in tears and tantrums.

We suggest putting Roxy in her safe, happy place. This could be a crate in another room. Once you have greeted all of your visitors, which is often filled with excitement, we can settle everyone down. When asked about if they can meet Roxy, let them know how you want them to greet her and supervise carefully. If you feel it may not go well, then it is best to say so and suggest a meet another day, maybe on a walk. Remember we do not wish Roxy to practice behaviour we do not want.

Your end goal may be to be able to take Roxy on a walk through a busy town where she will meet people, other dog and traffic while staying calm. Currently, this maybe makes Roxy anxious and she pulls on the leash, barks and lunges. Consider the question why do I want to do this? Do I need to do this? Could we do something else together instead? If this is going to be stressful why do it if we don't need to? Don't get swayed by the thoughts or advice from others.

Some people insist that she needs to just 'get used to it' and that, with repeated exposure, she will get better. This is unlikely to happen, her stress bucket is filling, she is repeating behaviour you don't want and she is being reinforced by doing that behaviour. In other words, she'll keep doing it, it is even likely to be such a negative experience that it gets worse. She is in 'sad land' and highly aroused, it can end in intense fear even rage. We'll talk more about the different styles of managing this in chapter 4.2.

Let's try a new scenario. We'll say that you want to be able to go to the pub with Roxy and have a meal, expecting her to lay down peacefully under your table whilst you eat. Currently though, she is restless, and she tries to jump up at your food. She may even be growling at other people or dogs.

First, consider why you want to go to the pub with her. Would she prefer to remain relaxing at home with a bone or long-lasting chew? Would she be safe, calm and happy at the pub? Keep her stress bucket in mind. Think about your motivation for taking her to the pub. Maybe you want to spend some time with her because you have been working all day?

That is understandable but do remember that Roxy needs lots of sleep and rest time. We do not have to entertain her more than a few hours a day. Any more than that and we may be adding to her stress bucket and over stimulating her. Consider, instead, spending thirty minutes doing some scent work or going on a short relaxing walk. Possibly just giving her a chew in her crate. You go out for your meal for a few hours and have a great relaxing time without worrying about Roxy's 'inappropriate' behaviour or what other people are thinking. You can then come home and play a few short games before you retire for the night.

Keep her in calm, 'happy land' with some positive excitement and enrichment activities. Question your thoughts on what is normal. Question your motivation for wanting something.

Ask yourself:

Why you should or shouldn't do something with Roxy or take her somewhere.

What can you do to maximise success with everything you do with Roxy?

How you can devise baby steps to build the confidence and expand the trust between you. Always keep in mind our 95% rule.

Meet Roxy's needs:

Reward Roxy's great choices when she follows your leash. This does not need to be with food, just let her know you are happy with her. Allow opportunities for Roxy to play with dogs she likes and who like her. She does not need to meet all dogs and be friends with them all. Supervise and manage the play and the environment. Keep it safe, calm and happy.

Roxy likes to work. Keep playing the games. Consider her breed and personality and think about appropriate activities for her. For example: a husky usually adores pulling and running with their team members, think about Bikejoring or dry land mushing. Consider other activities, such as swimming.

Roxy only need thirty to sixty minutes of hard, fast, fun, off leash exercise per day. Much of that can be done in a middle size garden.

> Note: Roxy does not need to go on a walk (or two) everyday as long as she is exercised appropriately and has plenty of enrichment in her life. She also does not need a meal in her food bowl once or twice a day. Look back to chapter 2.2. Ditch the bowl.

Remember how sensitive Roxy is to your position and posture. To your thoughts, emotions and behaviour. If you can teach Roxy to be attentive and responsive, for her to know the rules, life becomes so much easier. Practice patience at home with doorways, gateways and games. We like to go through the doorway first, not because we are expressing an alpha role, but because it is easier to keep several dogs calm if they are following us. At any one time we may have several Huskies, Jack Russells and Retriever puppies following us from where we have been working to the kitchen or to be released into the garden. It would be chaotic if we allowed them to all charge through the doorway together.

The excitement level would raise, they may forget their manners towards each other, it will likely not end well. The rule would be to wait patiently by the door. We do not necessarily ask for a sit, but you could. As long as we're waiting for calm. If one gets over excited, then we wait until they are calm.

It is a frequent lament that other members of the family may not take on board your new ideas and training. This can hold back the transformation, but you can still have your great relationship. Simply continue to role model, apply the new skills and techniques. The results will speak for themselves. You will need to be aware of the group stress bucket though.

Each time they start to charge around, simply do some calming activities. Just keep in mind that the majority of people are resistant to new ideas that challenge previous learning.

Taking turns with other dogs is a great way to teach patience and self-control. This may be something as simple as having the dogs sit and wait for a treat. Be consistent and communicate with congruent body language so Roxy can understand.

If you choose to go on a walk with Roxy keep it safe and set up for success. Try some of our earlier games for off-leash walking. Constantly take baby steps. Try the home first, then garden and then a quiet place. As always, stay present and focused yourself. If you are on your phone, you are not present or focused. Remember to put the value in proximity with Roxy staying by your side. Vary how you give Roxy treats. Sometimes feed her by your side instead of always sitting in front of you. Keep it flexible.

Keep Roxy safe by putting yourself in between Roxy and any hazard. It can be very powerful for you to put your back to the hazard (trigger). By doing this you are communicating that it is not important to you and does not require your attention. A hazard could be anything from other dogs to strangers. You will have practiced doing a reverse at home; where you quickly and calmly do an about turn to avoid confrontation in order to stop Roxy practicing an unwanted behaviour. This is a great strategy. Please do not feel you have 'bottled out'; you have kept Roxy safe and avoided the unwanted behaviour being practised. Remember Roxy will do what she has done before. She needs to learn a different behaviour in that situation.

Remember: Preventing the unwanted practice is an essential part of the training.

Be Roxy's advocate. Respect her emotions, pay attention, move away before she reacts, keep calm and confident. Stay present, focused and connected. The more attuned you are to Roxy and her needs, the better you communicate. The more confidence you give her, the more patience and responsiveness she will have.

Remember the question how long will it take? It is not Roxy's choice it is yours.

A Brief Case Study

Linda was struggling with Roxy, she wanted to compete in obedience classes and was considering gun dog classes, but she felt that Roxy was too inconsistent with her responses to commands. Linda knew that Roxy was keen to please but often simply rushed through a chain of behaviours until she hit upon the one that Linda had asked for. Linda reported that she felt Roxy was showing some fearful behaviour and would sometimes simply lie down and disengage from the session or she would collect a toy and chew it.

Upon discussion and after watching some interaction between the pair we believed Roxy was unable to decide which cue she should be paying attention to. Often Linda's body language and position were at variance with the verbal cue and task she was asking Roxy to perform. Since Roxy was paying attention to Linda's body language and eye contact, she was unable to complete the task.

When we worked simply with body language and no verbal cues Linda was amazed at how much Roxy could understand and comply. Once Linda realised how sensitive to her position, her energy level and mood she was able to regain the trust they had lost. Linda acknowledged that she would become frustrated when Roxy seemed to deliberately be doing the 'wrong' thing and she felt very disappointed when Roxy refused to train with her.

Once Linda realised that Roxy was confused and had not learned the verbal cues correctly, that she was struggling to get it right progress began to take place.

Initially games for confidence and relationship boosting were played together with no pressure or expectation. Games were kept very short. Linda ensured she was in a happy mood and resolved to just enjoy playing with Roxy. Within a week their relationship was hugely improved, with Roxy once again finding joy in interacting with Linda.

Once the fun, optimism and trust were back Roxy was able to learn the verbal cues and tasks. Linda now knows that if Roxy does not 'get it right' it is very likely that she simply didn't understand. This was important feedback for Linda who could then adjust her communication, make it easier and ensure her intention was clear.

Roxy and Linda have started to compete in obedience and aim to start with scent work classes soon.

Summary

In this chapter we have explored how to establish:

- Establishing a common language.
- Have you inadvertently taught your dog to ignore you?
- The mirror effect.
- Developing awareness for precision in your communication.
- Congruency.
- Patience
- Interactive dialogue loop.
- Being present – your position and posture.
- Intention
- Positive leadership
- Clarity

We imagine if you did not already know, you are starting to realise just how important you are, it is very easy for our communication to become muddled and unclear to our dogs. Often, we have not even taken the time to make our own thoughts clear. What do we want and why? Visualise what you do want. Keep your mind clear and stay in the moment. This is easier said than done, but like everything else it becomes easier with practice.

Mythbuster Moment: My dog does not listen to me.

It may seem as if your dog is not listening, indeed you may have inadvertently taught her to ignore you at times. However, if you work on giving very clear, consistent, congruent communication with your full focus this can change and your dog will listen to you. Remember communication is two way – you need to listen to her too.

In this chapter we briefly mentioned the pitfall of having a permissive parenting style, we advocate being a compassionate leader who is calm and confident. Being a loving leader, a great parent. We are aware that often people believe that using positive reinforcement as a training approach will not give real life results and when faced with what we see as a problem or a severe behavioural issue we often turn to a more assertive, punishment based approach where we are informed we need to be the alpha and dominate our dog. This may be tempting as it often seems like it will be a quick fix. We will explore this approach in more detail in the next chapter, giving reasons as to why we should reconsider.

ALPHA STYLE IS OLD STYLE

A discussion of the old style of Alpha dominance
training and positive reinforcement training.

- Alpha Dominance approach – Busted
- Positive reinforcement training.

A brief testimonial of Xina, a female Malamute.

"Having owned dogs for 40 years, I was taught that you needed to be the boss, that you could expect to sometimes have to assert your dominance. I have never been happy doing this and am delighted to find that science does not support it either. My husband tells me that I have to be the boss and points to the fact that Xina, my Malamute, behaves better for him. I have realised that she's actually showing some signs of anxiety with him. Now I have started with the games and that I understand about being a loving leader I have found she listens and cooperates with me beautifully. All without any intimidation. Our relationship has blossomed."

The Alpha Dominance approach

We have previously mentioned that we have a team of around fourteen Huskies at any one time, sometimes more if we have recently taken on a new Husky that needed re-homing. The most common question, often the first one we are asked is, 'do they [the Huskies] see you as pack leader? Are you the Alpha?'

This is not surprising as there are still many internet sites about dominating your dog, books, blogs, tv shows, vets, trainers and behaviour professionals that do still subscribe to this theory. They state that the human must be the Alpha. In a family, humans, including children must be first. They must have a higher ranking than the dog. They may instruct you to use force and intimidation to overpower Xina into submission.

Such ideas become a powerful social construct, easy to get a hold of. It seems like it is a good idea as we like to think that we are top of the evolutionary tree.

Often specific dogs are given the label of dominant. This is not a correct use of the work dominant. It should only be used in context, and in comparison with another. For example, if Xina growls or shows her teeth, perhaps if there is a high value toy/treat, and gives signs associated with dominance and the other dog moves away, maybe even rolls over and shows behaviour associated with submission. We are likely to give Xina the label of dominant. In reality, the word is only valid in comparison with another who is more submissive. In one scenario Xina only be dominant on that particular day with that particular context. This can change, either with a different dog. or perhaps with a different resource under which circumstance she may be the submissive dog.

Given what you have already learned this will not surprise you. Remember to consider the context. Think about how full their stress buckets are and how motivated Xina is towards the goal. Some days she may just let Fifi have the goal rather than bothering to assert herself.

Often, the switches can often be more to do with confidence rather than if an individual is more dominant than the other in the given context. Remember behaviour driven by anxiety can be mis-interpreted as dominance. This mistaken approach to canine social behaviour, known as Dominance Theory, is based on a study of captive wolves in the '30s and '40s by Rudolph Schenkel. He concluded that wolves in a pack fight to gain dominance, the winner being the Alpha wolf.

Erroneously, this conclusion was extrapolated to wild wolves. Sadly, the mistake has now been widely accepted. The captured wolves were all previously unknown to each other, they were in a stressful situation of being captive with scarce resources. It is known that animals, including humans, are likely to fight under such circumstances. In the wild the wolf pack is likely to consist of the breeding pair and their young. The older mature offspring leaving the group to seek their own mate.

In captivity adult wolves are forced to live together, in a restricted space, with scarce resources. Thus, creating tension which would not be the case in the wild group.

Further, the Dominance Theory was based on wolves and not dogs. Dogs are not wolves. They have evolved differently and have been selectively bred to fulfil specific functions in partnership with humans. In an earlier chapter we discussed how a wolf's neocortex (the clever bit) is bigger than a dog's neocortex. The wolf needs to be able to plan to survive.

The thought is that wolves live in hierarchical packs (Alpha, beta etc.) and since dogs are descended from wolves, the human needs to be the Alpha over the dog. There are many flaws with the reasoning – not to mention the original theory based on the flawed research was erroneous.

Sadly, this idea really did and continues to hold the imagination. The military has expounded this concept. William Koehler trained dogs for the military prior to training civilian dogs. He advocated hanging, helicoptering a dog into submission, into unconsciousness if necessary, so as to stop a dog from digging. He suggested filling the hole with water and submerging the dogs head into the water filled hole until she was nearly drowned.

In 1978 The Monks of New Skete, which was the then cutting edge of dog training, were advocated as, 'understanding being the key to communication, compassion and communion'. Whilst they formulated the 'Alpha wolf role' where the dog is forced physically onto their side and held there.

This was taken from the observation of this behaviour in captive wolves. This was misinterpreted. It can be confused with the voluntary submissive roll over by the less assertive dog. Not forcibly commanded by stronger ones. This Alpha role is still being widely used and recommended by some dog trainers. It was also advocated to use other physical punishments such as the scruff shake, lifting the dog of the ground and hitting under the chin several times hard enough to cause a yelp.

This was all done while professing that, 'training dogs is about building a relationship that is based on respect and love and understanding'. They advocate a gentle, kindly look tells the dog she is loved and accepted; they also state it is vital to communicate a stern reaction to bad behaviour.

A piercing sustained stare into a dog's eyes tells her who is in charge, it establishes the proper hierarchy of dominance between person and pet. Remember back to 1.4 on body language communication. It may elicit a strong aggressive response if you chose the wrong dog for that sustained stare. It may also make the timid, anxious dog more anxious.

The above dominance theory is still alive and well, though the knowledge that it is a myth is gradually becoming more mainstream. It is unnecessary, and potentially damaging.

Positive Reinforcement training

Karen Pryor wrote her seminal book 'don't shoot the dog' in 1985 when dominance-based training was still going strong. She was a marine mammal trainer using the principles of classical and operant conditioning as introduced by the fathers of behavioural psychology Pavlov, Watson and Skinner. The knowledge was available from 1930s about how animals could be effectively trained, without dominance. This theory was not applied to dogs until Karen Pryor's book. In 1993 the veterinary behaviourist, Dr Ian Dunbar, founded the association of pet dog trainers (APDT). This approach promotes the use of reward based training methods, minimizing the use of aversive techniques.

With advances in positive training and increasingly educated dog training profession embracing the science of behaviour and learning the pain causing abusive methods such as the Alpha roll, scruff shake, hanging, drowning and cuffing has decreased.

Dominance theory experienced a come-back in popularised T.V. shows and seems, at first sight, to offer a quick, easy fix to struggles such as 'dogs labelled as reactive or aggressive'. In truth, such harsh methods using force are known in scientific learning theory terms as 'positive punishment' and are part of operant conditioning theory. These methods can work at shutting down behaviour and convincing a dog that it is not safe to do anything unless instructed to do something.

This can lead to Xina always trying to work out what is needed to avoid punishment and being stressed. It may seem to work with some dogs, but not so much with others.

Dogs that are resilient enough to withstand the punishment, but not so tough and assertive that they fight back, may cope without obvious fallout.

With a dog likely to fight back, then the struggle escalates and is likely to be dangerous. They may submit for the moment but may erupt aggressively the next time. Such dogs are deemed unsafe, not suitable and may be euthanized.

On the other hand, the soft, sensitive dog can be easily psychologically damaged by dominance training. This dog shuts down and becomes fearful and mistrusting, believing humans to be unpredictable and unfairly violent. Please remember that the stressed, fearful Xina cannot learn. If you are then trying to train her, even using positive reinforcement, you may not get the results you seek. You may believe Xina is being stubborn, is not very intelligent or any other thought you choose to believe. The reality is that trust needs to be built first, with no pressure on Xina.

Please, if you have used the dominance type of training and now realise it can be very harmful,don't feel bad. Yes, it would be great to go back and redo all that training and have a better understanding with our previous dogs. To give them a less stressful life, one with even more joy than you had together. However, we cannot go back. Ditch those negative thoughts and move forward. When we know better, we do better. We are learning all the time. Norms change.

Successful social groups work because of voluntary deference, not because of aggressively enforced dominance. The whole point of social body language rituals is to avoid conflict and confrontation, not to cause it. Spend time watching a group of dogs, they will defer to each other, but it is not the same dogs that defer all the time.

Social hierarchies do exist in groups of domesticated dogs and the hierarchy can be fluid. It depends on what is at stake, and how strongly each dog feels about the outcome.

Social animals do understand hierarchy, they have their needs as discussed in previous chapters. We can use this information to be their loving leader, not 'the intimidating scary person'. They will choose to respect, trust and follow our suggestions since we make great decisions while always giving them a good deal. They do understand our emotions and our body language, often much better than we do. If we can give great leadership vibes, alongside using the science of behaviour and provide for Xina's needs all will come together quickly. The previous struggles will turn into strengths.

Simply hoping things will eventually get better as Xina becomes older, or as she gets used to things, is unlikely to change the struggle. Remember if she is being rewarded, i.e. feeling better when she is barking, enjoying running off and chasing, then she will continue with this behaviour.

You are the catalyst for change.

A Brief Case Study

Jackie attended the consultation with Xina, Paul and Jackie had owned dogs for over forty years. Though this was their first Malamute. Linda was concerned that she was finding it increasingly difficult to walk Xina. In the past they had been able to train their previous dogs to walk to heel upon request. Xina would not walk to heel with either Linda or Paul without using strong and repeated correction. Linda reported that on a back-clip harness she was unable to hold Xina's power. She knew that using the collar and allowing Xina to pull in front was likely to cause damage to Xina's neck and still found that even if she used a choke type chain, or martingale she still struggled to hold Xina and know that she had control.

Xina had almost zero recall even at home. She was beginning to show reactivity on her walks, pulling even harder when she saw other dog and becoming particularly over-excited and vocal if she saw other animals. Under these circumstances she would not listen to either Linda or Paul.

Linda and Paul had read up on the characteristics of the breed and did not let her off the leash unless in a secure area. As she became older, she was increasingly more difficult to catch and put back on the leash when it was time to finish. Linda admitted that they had not been to the off-leash areas for a couple of months so Xina was only getting on-leash walks.

Linda initially said that Xina did seem to pay more attention to Paul who did sometimes use punishment and very strong, harsh tone and correction. Linda felt she was never able to use a

similar strategy and felt she lacked the ability to dominate Xina as Paul felt was necessary. Linda reported that she did shout at Xina and utilised time out strategies but felt that Xina still paid no attention to her.

During the consultation the power of fun games was discussed. Linda stated that Xina had no interest in balls, toys, sticks etc. She was not hugely food motivated often leaving her food and refusing dog treats. Linda was at a loss to know how to train a dog who had no interest in toys or treats. Linda believed games would not work since she could give no effective reward.

Ditch the bowl was discussed together with the power of the seeking drive. Linda was concerned that given she often left her food that she would not work for it. The power of activating the food, rolling it along the floor to activate Xina's chase drive was demonstrated. Scent games were demonstrated using a higher value, strong smelling food. Linda was reassured that often northern breeds chose to not eat for a few days especially in the warmer months. Often these breeds become bored very quickly, so games have to be short with very few repetitions and move on to another one.

Treats from the sky was a powerful motivator for Xina using high value treats, Linda was then able to attain some loose leash walking. All the wombling games were introduced and practiced, walking slowly and then speeding up. By frequent changes of direction and pace, practicing giving in to leash pressure, Linda became more confident of being able to walk Xina. It was suggested that Linda and Xina drove to suitable quiet places where they could practice together with few distractions.

A head halter was discussed, with the cone games to help Xina have positive associations. Xina was a very confident girl and had no problem with cone games and harness but did have a history of using her paws to remove head halters. Keeping her distracted when wearing it and keeping her paws moving was demonstrated with the reminder to have the session short and rewarding. Once Xina was comfortable wearing a head halter Linda felt more confident that she could hold her power if it became necessary. Linda also purchased and introduced a front clip harness, though Paul continued to use the collar.

Linda was the person who had given Xina her meals, so it was easy for her to change how she delivered the food using games to build up the desire for proximity, recall and their relationship.

Linda was much more comfortable with the concept of building the relationship so Xina chose to listen rather than use force and intimidation.

As Linda's confidence grew and she felt Xina would listen she was able to start going out for regular walks. She noticed that Xina now listened to her much more readily than she did to Paul. Xina's body language was more joyful when interacting with Linda and more subdued when following Paul's commands.

Summary

In this chapter we discussed the Be the Alpha, dominance style of leadership and pointed out the damage that can be caused. Clearly it is aversive and can be abusive.

- The Alpha, dominance approach creates chronic stress which is not helpful to training, our dog's wellbeing and our partnership. It can seem to give a quick fix, which is tempting, but it does not address the root of the struggle. Our dog continues to feel the emotional pain, learns not to react and to suffer it quietly. This can take the form of a learned helplessness. Or the dog may choose to react with rage as the struggle changed from anxiety to fear to rage as it intensified.
- There is a difference between being a great parent, a loving leader and an over strict punitive parent who does not listen.

We've also talked about the Positive Reinforcement approach.

- We do advocate a positive reinforcement- based approach but our approach is so much more. We realise that to have real life results holding out a food reward may not be enough. We realise that we do need to take control, to manage the environment as well.
- Simply ignoring the behaviour (as often advocated with this approach) will not necessarily make it stop. In fact, if it a rewarding behaviour in itself it will definitely be repeated. Each time it is practiced the behaviour chain is stronger. Our dog will feel safe, happy and calm if they can trust us to be a great loving leader; One who keeps them safe so they do not have to struggle.

Mythbuster Moment: you need to be the boss, to be the Alpha

This is simply not true. You do not need to intimidate your dog. This approach can be harmful and very detrimental to your relationship.

In the next chapter we will explore further just how deep the connection with our dog can be, both biologically and energetically. We discuss how we may inadvertently be the block preventing our dog from reaching their best self. Not something you want to hear. Often our motives and compassion are pure, but we lack the knowledge, skill and insight. This is a case for your dog not being the dog you imagined but the dog you needed for self-growth.

MUTUAL HEALTH AND MENTAL WELLBEING

CHAPTER INTRODUCTION:

Looking at the connection between you, your mental
and physical health and the health of your dog.

- Connection of health.
- Entrainment and shared biological states.
- Your health and wellbeing.
- Research and evidence for the link between thought, emotion and behaviour.
- Mindfulness and living in the moment.
- Ditch the label of 'Rescue'.
- Reframing your negative thoughts.
- Perceived control and reducing stress.
- Identifying the automatic thoughts and emotions experienced.

A brief testimonial of Jet, a female Spaniel/Pointer cross.

"At first I felt guilty that so many of Jet's problems were perhaps coming from me. That she was mirroring my anxiety. But, with help, I realised that feeling guilty was not helpful either. Once I realised that I could change things for the better I began to do so. I now regularly meditate and practice positive reframing of my thoughts. I can now see how my dog mirrors me; When she is showing anxiety it actually makes me pause to check my thoughts, emotions and body language. She is such a great teacher. I am getting better at having a more optimistic outlook but it's definitely a work in progress. Jet, on the other hand, is streets ahead of me for progress. By following Sonia's advice, she is much more optimistic, calm and confident."

Connection of Health

We know that we are not alone when we say that we have noticed a connection between the health of Jet and the health of the person they are most strongly bonded with. Have you ever heard it said that many dogs and humans look alike and have similar personalities? Much of this is based on anecdotal evidence given the difficulties of scientific study, not to mention the cost and ethical implications.

Several vets and holistic care practitioners have noted and commented on the above. Around 50% of the time the health issue presenting in Jet has its mirror in her carer. This statement could leash to the carer/parent feeling guilty, but it is in no way the fault of the person. Ditch the guilt, it adds to your stress which is not helpful to Jet.

Jet and friends are empathetic. Empathy is the natural sensory phenomenon, whereby one being experiences the feelings of another in their own sensory awareness. Think of you watching horror movies and feeling the fear of the protagonist or crying when watching a sorrowful scene. Jet knows how you are feeling, happy, sad, anxious, angry, frustrated... You get the picture. With this in mind, it is no surprise that if you have anxiety, Jet feels it. Over time this may lead to her becoming, like you; a being with anxiety.

Entrainment

This is when any two systems with patterns of vibration will tend to synchronise with each other. This can be demonstrated by placing mechanical pendulum clocks on the same table. Within a short space of time they come into harmony and tick together.

This has also been demonstrated with heart rate. Changes in heart rate between strongly bonded people and other beings synchronise. This is known as Heart Rate Variability synchronization. There is a spontaneous synchronisation of other body rhythms too. Whether they are healthy or unhealthy.

We can have shared biological states with Jet driven by a combination of empathy and electromagnetic entrainment. The heart is the primary driver of the electromagnetic field which extends beyond the physical body.

There are stories everywhere for when Jet has known when their bonded partner is coming home and shows excitement before they arrive. This is even when predictability factors, such as the time of day, or their superior sense of smell or hearing is accounted for. You may have experienced similar with either your pet or another loved one.

Research by Rupert Sheldrake supports that it is indeed something other than the explanations given by routine, hearing the vehicle, picking up the behaviour from other humans as a clue, selective reporting bias etc. Anecdotal evidence also provides examples of anticipatory behaviour within other species; Closely bonded horses often show this behaviour upon the imminent return of their partner. This may be even when the other horse is traveling in horse-transport several miles away with no routine time return.

If we accept that the physiological synchronization is a result of a close, loving, trusting relationship with another being, it follows that the healthier you become physically, spiritually, mentally and emotionally the healthier your dog will become. Please consider you own health first.

We often find we are happy to work hard on our loved ones' health and wellbeing whilst being careless of our own. Consider changing this. This can be hard, as we are often hard on ourselves. Think about your personal growth and health. Work towards improving it. Maybe your motivation comes from knowing the healthier you are emotionally, spiritually and physically the more helpful it is to your loved ones. We will often do things for others and are kinder to them than we are to ourselves. Many ancient philosophies and wisdom do stress the idea of healing yourself first, then helping others.

In addition to tracing a link between the physical health of Jet and her carer, we have explored the connection on a mental and emotional level. In discussing mirroring, we see how the humans' emotions and body language is mirrored by Jet. The carer who lives in an anxious mindset can lead to Jet having a similar anxious mindset.

This is not invariable, remember the individual personality. Some dogs are inherently calm, confident and are less likely to take on the anxiety. We often say many family dogs are successful and remain calm because they can ignore 90% of the messages from the human. Working for many years with horses we have noticed that the so-called 'bomb proof' horses had just learnt to ignore 90% of the human communication and have become victims of learned helplessness; particularly with riding school horses who were at the receiving end of hugely conflicting commands from their handler. The novice would pull the reins as a signal to stop at the same time as using the legs to send the horse forwards or give a right turn signal with reins whilst giving the opposing command with the legs. The horse just did as little as possible and tended to go on autopilot, following other horses and maybe simply listening to the instructors' commands.

If we are motivated to be in the best physical health in order to help Jet, it makes sense that we need also to consider our thoughts, our emotions and our behaviour. You may have heard of cognitive behaviour therapy. This is to help recognise and control our negative thoughts, which link to negative emotions and behaviour and keep circling on a downward negative spiral; perhaps into anxiety, panic attack or, depression.

It is important to note that we are not our thoughts, our brain is there to help us process information. Simply because we have a thought or belief, it does not mean it is true. We can change that thought and replace it with another. This sounds simple and in theory it is. In practice, however, it is far more difficult. Humans are creatures of habit and feel comfortable with previously learned patterns of thinking and behaviour. We need to be incredibly motivated in order to change. But change we can.

Mindfulness

By this point, you can identify a recurring theme. We must identify our thoughts, be self-aware and honest about how we are feeling. We need to notice the frustration or anxiety and learn self- help techniques to interrupt the negative cycle. We can do this by replacing it with a reframed, more positive thought and emotion.

We discussed in chapter 3.2, how some dogs are more pessimistic in their judgement bias. No surprise that this applies to humans too. Are you the glass half full or half empty person? Given motivation to change we can also learn to be more optimistic. To change from half empty to half full, just like our dogs. It is easier to shape Jets personality than ours because Jet lives more in the moment and is not worrying about what will happen tomorrow. She is not ruminating on what happened yesterday.

Humans find it difficult to live in the moment. Our modern life, stresses or work tend to mean we are always thinking and planning ahead. However, we can still practice mindfulness and spend time living in the moment. We can utilise time with Jet as our living in the moment time. This will mean our communication and our relationship with her will skyrocket. She will be overjoyed to receive your full attention. If we are fully present with her, she will respond by being attentive and responsive to you.

When we say Jet lives more in the moment, we do not mean that she has no memory of the past, clearly, she does. What we are saying is that she is not likely to be ruminating with negative thoughts in the same way a human may. As far as we know she is not likely to be worrying about what may happen on her walk later. We do know that Jet can suffer PTSD type symptoms which demonstrate just how traumatic she has found elements of her previous life. Being rehomed can, for some dogs, be traumatic enough to be associated with subsequent PTSD.

Ditch the label of rescue dog

Sadly, being rehomed is likely to be traumatic so we need to be aware of Jet's needs, but guard against keeping her in a negative emotional state by your projection of how sad you feel for her. Both of you need practice living in the moment and ditch the label of rescue dog whenever we say Jet is a rescue dog, it is likely to remind us of her previous circumstances and emotional state. In discussing it further with other people it plays a loop in our head which is likely to send us to a negative emotional state. We may begin feeling sad for Jet, angry with people in her previous life etc. This is then possibly mirrored back by Jet.

Unless you absolutely know you can state Jet is a rescue dog without any negative thoughts and emotions about that, then best not to say it. Do people need to know? Often, we can use this as an explanation of why Jet is behaving as she is especially if she is exhibiting behaviour that embarrasses us.

Reframing your negative thoughts

Sonia's qualifications and work in teaching people with special needs and especially people with mental health issues such as anxiety, panic attacks and depression has clearly shown the link between negative thinking, negative emotions and negative behaviour. Studies in psychology which include cognitive behavioural therapy, Neuro-Linguistic Programming, Sports Psychology and Mindfulness all demonstrate this link. We do not propose to go into detail here but do encourage you to investigate.

We do not suggest that you have any negative mental health issue. Though it is more 'normal' than you may know. Studies have shown 48% of people do have at least one episode of mental health issue at some time in their life. What we do suggest is that you should be aware of what you are thinking, monitor your thoughts. If you notice it is framed in a negative way, then re-frame the thought to a positive mindset. You are not your thoughts; they are there to help you navigate life. This takes practice and you may need help.

Many studies show that we put blocks on our own progress, such blocks are not real they are simply how we have interpreted life events and how we imagine future life events. It all sounds very simple, but it really does take practice. Just like any change we may need to work at it. It can be easy to slip back into previous patterns of thinking, feeling and behaving. Like any new skill it becomes easier with practice, methods such as meditation, relaxation exercises will all help. Our thoughts may block our dog's progress to be their best self.

Think about your own stress bucket and how you can manage this to keep it empty or empty it more quickly. Again, just as you can help Jet learn to cope better with frustration and be more optimistic, you can learn techniques to help yourself.

Exercise has been shown to be very beneficial at helping cope with stress. If you use your walks with Jet as your exercise but find that you are having negative associations with the walk and worrying about encounters with other dogs etc then this is not going to be stress reducing for you. So, consider other exercise without Jet or in a location which is safe, calm and happy for you both.

Control of your environment and your life

Considerable research has been published which demonstrates the link between perceived control and good mental and physical health. Be proactive about your life, be creative with your solutions to things that previously you thought could not be changed. You may have to make small changes whilst you are working towards a bigger change but simply moving in the right direction will be hugely motivating and will reduce the level of your own stress bucket.

When we look at psychological theories please remember they are theories with some evidence gathered in the scientific manner to support them. It can be very confusing. But there seems no doubt of the strong connection between thoughts, emotions and behaviour. Whichever comes first and 'causes' the other is not the important issue, the thing to do is step in and break any negative spiral.

The first step is being aware of the thought, the emotion and the behaviour. We can learn to control our behaviour by using methods such as meditative and relaxation techniques. We can control our thoughts by identifying the negative thought and reframing to a positive thought. Our emotions are tied in so closely with thoughts and behaviour that controlling them will change our emotion. Recognise the anxiety and negative stress, consider inappropriate and unhelpful thoughts. practice mindfulness and techniques to reduce bodily tension.

Learning to identify automatic thoughts can be very interesting and identifying them will help you understand why you feel the way you feel in different situations. The more attention you pay to your thoughts, the easier it is to identify several thoughts tied to a mood/emotion.

Do more of what helps you to be calm and happy. Take control of your environment, make changes to set yourselves up for success. Remember perceived control reduces stress for both you and Jet. Listen to her communication, maybe she is not feeling safe? Change the situation, take the baby steps towards having her feel happy in the environment currently causing her stress. Consider before doing that: why is it necessary for her to change? Why is it necessary for you to change? Is it necessary at all?

There is no normal in this, you are both perfect as you are. If it makes you happy to be motivated towards a specific carefully chosen goal. then set off with baby steps towards achieving your goal.

You will probably have heard of SMART; specific, measurable, achievable, realistic and time sensitive targets. This may be a technique you will find useful in breaking your overall goal into baby steps. Many people like to have worksheets, written plans and feel hugely motivated as progress can be measured. You can then track how far you have travelled in your journey. Personally, we find the process creates 'work' and pulls us away from living in the moment. Try it and see if it suits you and helps you make measurable progress on your journey.

Life is a journey, make the journey safe, calm and happy. Enjoy.

Mind, Consciousness, and Thought.

In the 70's Syd Banks proposed that the mind is the intelligence of all things; Consciousness makes you aware; and thought is like the rudder of a ship. It guides you through life, and if you learn to use that rudder properly, you can guide your way through life far better than you ever imagined. You can go from one reality to another. You can find your happiness and when illusionary sadness comes from memories, you don't try to figure it out. All you must do is realize that it's Thought. The second you realize that it's Thought, you are touching the very essence of psychological experience. You're back in the 'now' you're back into happiness. So, don't get caught up on the details.

We're going to delve a little more into spirituality now. Everyone is equal when it comes to the spirit. It doesn't matter where you are, or even who you are. Everybody has spiritual knowledge and they don't realise it. Sometimes someone will say something that triggers something in you, even without them knowing it. There's no human being more spiritual than you, everybody is equal.

The true equaliser for us is that we all derive from Mind, Consciousness, and Thought. While you have that equalizer, you're as good as anybody on this Earth. You always have been, always will be; the only thing is, you don't see it because of your thoughts.

In summary, everything we experience in life is a function of these spiritual facts: we are alive, we are aware, and we think. We are only ever one new thought away from a completely different experience of being alive.

Wittgenstein stated that, 'A man will be imprisoned in a room with a door that's unlocked and opens inwards as long as it does not occur to him to pull rather than push'

Experience is not coming at us from the outside in, it is coming through us from the inside and is expressed to the outside in our emotions and behaviour. We are living in the feeling of our thinking, not the feeling of the world. Reality changes when viewed from different levels of understanding. The more we understand where our experience comes from the less anxious, we will be.

When our thoughts look real, we may live in a world of suffering. When they look subjective, we live in a world of choice. When they look arbitrary, we live in a world of possibility and when we see them as illusory, we wake up in a world of dreams.

We are sure you have all seen posts and memes that tell us that we are our own enemy. That we are holding ourselves back and being the block on our dreams. William James believes that, 'most people live, whether physically, intellectually, or morally, in a very restricted circle of their potential being.'

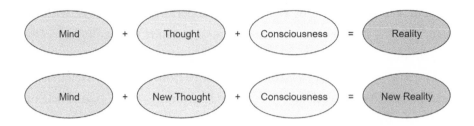

Insights change our world. An insight is a new thought, containing information and wisdom outside our current knowledge. In order to have these insights we do need to slow down with our thoughts, to still the mind. This is probably why meditation works so well to promote mental and physical health. It is the gateway to wisdom and opens up a world of deeper feelings and gives glimpses into the nature of the universe.

It has become very popular in western culture over the last sixty years and has been standard practice in Eastern and Oceanic culture for several Millenia. There is a difference between employing meditative techniques and being in a meditative state of mind. You need to slow down your thoughts.

When our mind is empty, it can be filled with insight from the natural intelligence that exists beyond our personal thinking. This is our innate wisdom. When we listen without anything on our mind, we become receptive to that wisdom. Meditation, a quiet mind and a beautiful feeling is our natural state. The less we have on our mind, the better life gets.

There is now so much information via the internet that it is easy to become overwhelmed and unsure of quite what to believe. We have an inbuilt cognitive bias to simply believe what we want to believe. This helps us to simplify our world. Consider being open minded.

We still struggle with some aspects of the spiritual information that we have discovered. Though, we do continue to read and consider if it may be 'true'. This is probably because of a more traditional and scientific background, in which, when we have a hypothesis, we must put it to a rigorous scientific test with experimentation/observation and so on. Applying statistical tests to the results to see if the hypothesis is supported or not.

Happily, what we do know is that there is now more scientific research that does support the spiritual element of the world and the more seemingly 'outlandish' ideas. For us, we can be held back by knowing that we may experience something but then our analytical thoughts can step in and question it. Especially knowing that we may perceive what we are motivated to perceive. This may resonate with you.

With this book simply take out the parts that resonate and motivate you, consider your journey of growth, maybe later some other aspects introduced in the next chapter may resonate and you will investigate further.

A Brief Case Study

Susan came for a consultation with Jet, her six-year-old female spaniel/pointer. Susan described Jet as very anxious, reluctant to settle, seeking attention constantly and full of energy. Susan found it difficult to meet the exercise levels she felt Jet needed. She has owned Jet since a pup of eight weeks and always hoped she would eventually settle down and not be 'quite so manic all the time'.

At the beginning of the consultation it was apparent that we would find it difficult to take a detailed case history since both Susan and Jet were distracted, with very scattered attention. It was decided to go on a walk to discuss the issues Susan wished to address. It was a very similar picture outside on the walk. Jet was lively and tense, Susan was constantly verbally correcting Jet, using very high energy corrections and body language, her tension and anxiety was very apparent. After a twenty-minute walk, it was suggested that Jet go for a walk with one of us (as Susan felt Jet would not settle in her car or a crate) whilst they discussed their struggles.

Susan described herself as prone to worry, found it hard to simply relax, preferred to keep busy as she often felt guilty if she was doing nothing. She walked Jet for up to four hours each day, tried to meet Jet's need for constant attention by playing games such as fetch. She said Jet would chase a ball all day, no matter how long they had played, Jet always wanted more and would bark at Susan to get her to continue with the game. Susan often responded to the barking by more game playing.

During the consultation the stress buckets were discussed together with the amount of sleep and rest a dog actually needed. The calmness procedure was discussed at length together with ditch the bowl and routine. Jet had been crate trained as a pup and would sometimes go into her crate to sleep though Susan never shut the door.

Owing to the very high level of tension Susan was showing, some considerable length of time was spent discussing Susan's personality and worries. Sonia described how dogs can often mirror human emotions. Susan immediately saw that Jet was being influenced by Susan's emotional state. She noted how much calmer Jet was in the company of Susan's friend and dog sitter. We discussed meditation techniques and practiced reframing. Susan was given a journal to complete. Other relaxations techniques were discussed briefly with Susan being given links for further information and useful resources.

Susan requested follow-up coaching calls with regular email correspondence. Susan was also given documents to download to help explain why plenty of rest, less exciting physical exercise and more activities that require using Jet's brain and nose implemented instead. Susan was instructed to simply play the calming games and implement the calmness procedure for three days, no ball play or exciting games and to teach Jet the rudiments of scent work games. For two weeks to only go out on short walks using plenty of 'wombling around' activities.

Within a week, Susan reported Jet was settling down much more quickly. She found that if she meditated with Jet next to her, Jet would relax quickly. Susan started to do three-minute meditations throughout the day in conjunction with giving Jet a long-lasting chew in her crate. She found that Jet would then simply go to sleep afterwards.

Three weeks later Susan felt Jet was transformed. It had become more apparent that if Susan could remain calm then Jet found it easy to be calm too. Now Jet's stress bucket was kept below threshold with less high excitement activity and plenty of sleep Jet was able to settle quickly and was not demanding attention.

Susan was shown how to give Jet a calming massage, she was also shown how to select aromatherapy oils and check that Jet gave her consent to treatment. She found that giving the massage was as relaxing as Jet found receiving it. This effect was heightened with the playing of soothing music. The oils, music and soothing, slow massage strokes helped both to relax. Jet was so in tune with Susan that she very quickly mirrored Susan's emotional state.

Jet is much calmer, more optimistic and confident in general and only becomes stressed and anxious when Susan is particularly anxious. Susan knows she can simply go to the calmness procedure for Jet and give her time in her crate. Jet will then settle down and sleep.

Summary

In this chapter we have discussed:

- Connection of health.
- Entrainment and shared biological states.
- Your health and wellbeing.
- Research and evidence for the link between thought, emotion and behaviour.
- Mindfulness and living in the moment.
- Ditch the label of 'Rescue'.
- Reframing your negative thoughts.
- Perceived control and reducing stress.
- Identifying the automatic thoughts and emotions experienced.

Mythbuster Moment: my dog is a rescue who was abused, he missed out on socialisation when he was a puppy, he will always be reactive as he is now.

Unless your dog has a medical condition that is driving his behaviour, we can shape his personality, gain calmness and through games teach alternative behaviour. Ditch those negative thoughts or they become the reality.

This is a lot to take in, to consider and to move forward. Keeping a journal will help keep you on track and motivate you to continue your journey. Enjoy the journey, it can be the seeking, the anticipation that is most rewarding for us. Even more so than achieving the final goal.

In the next chapter we will discuss Holistic Therapies to help enhance your partnership.

4.4

HOLISTIC TOOLS

CHAPTER INTRODUCTION:

A very brief introduction of some Holistic Therapies which will help alleviate your dog's stress and boost your relationship.

- Aromatherapy and essential oils.
- Flower essences.
- Herbal treatment.
- Acupuncture, Acupressure, Shiatzu and Red-Light therapy.
- The Heart Connection.

A brief testimonial of a six-dog household.

"I am so blown away by how effective holistic therapies are with dogs. I have a household of 6 rescue dogs. I have in the last 6 months started to add some aromatherapy, flower essences and herbal preparations to the weekly routine. Sonia's guidance has been brilliant, since she's met my dogs. We gradually added different treatments for each dog.

I keep records of everything I use and have observation sheets. With that feedback I may adjust the dose or product. The integration with gentle massage and stroking and some simple acupressure techniques has led to phenomenal results. I am so happy and love this approach. I had not previously used such therapies even with myself but now am totally convinced and yes, I use them myself now too."

For our final chapter, we want to move towards integrating methods for individual dogs in individual circumstances. When working on a specific struggle, we must tailor it to the specific dog. We always work with the dog front of us.

As you learn new things, don't walk away from what you learned in the past. See if you can mould an even better individually tailored approach, for the right dog with the right handler at the right time. If we are working on reactivity, we also work on overall arousal levels. The stress bucket is always relevant and playing selected games helps immensely. We need to consider how we are affecting our Fido. Is he mirroring us? Or are we adding to his anxiety?

We can also use natural remedies and holistic healthcare as complementary options. This way, Fido can enjoy a long, happy and healthy life. Think about using an integrative approach. This means you are more likely to learn new things and add dramatically to your skill base.

Rarely is there a right or a wrong approach, instead look for a good approach for the circumstances. Integrate that with all that you know and recognise that other combinations may well have worked just as well. There is a wide range of holistic and natural remedies that can be used to help. You may be familiar with some but have not considered using them for Fido. You will need to do some research to check that the product is safe for dogs, pregnant dogs etc.

Aromatherapy and essential oils

This is not limited to the use of grooming products that contain essential oils. It refers to the use of a Pure essential oil or several oils combined, for a certain healing purpose. Examples may include helping to control a specific health problem, enhance overall wellbeing or help with a behavioural struggle. Do not try to save money and buy cheap essential oils, you need to do your research and buy 100% pure oils from a reputable source.

An essential oil is a volatile substance contained in the glandular hairs, sac, or veins of different parts of a plant. They are the essence of that particular plant form and responsible for giving the unique scent.

There are several ways to extract the essential oils. Essential oils are highly concentrated and should almost always be diluted before use. Each oil has its own properties, such as scent, colour, chemical properties and healing effects.

On a physical level, many essential oils are antibacterial, anti-viral, anti-fungal, anti-inflammatory and detoxifying. On an emotional level, some essential oils can be relaxing or stimulating.

A hydrosol is a water-based substance which is a by-product obtained during the steam distillation process of an essential oil. A hydrosol contains water soluble parts of a plant as well as very small amount of some essential oil components. Since hydrosols are not highly concentrated like essential oils, they can be used undiluted, or essential oils can be added to a hydrosol for synergistic effects. For extremely sensitive dogs, hydrosols are good alternative to the more potent essential oils.

Are essential oils safe for dogs? You should always be careful. The oils always need to be diluted with a carrier oil such as olive oil, sweet almond oil etc. Again, always bear in mind that all dogs are different and may react very differently even to the same oil. Go slowly and observe carefully.

Unsafe oils include anise, camphor, hyssop, juniper, white thyme and yarrow. Especially on pregnant dogs. Beware also of using birch or wintergreen for joint pains caused by arthritis. Dermal use of these two oils have been shown to be toxic as they contain high levels of methyl salicylate. Ingestion can cause poisoning. Cassia, clover leaf and bud can cause dermal irritation and possible toxicity. Horseradish, mustard and tansy are also considered to be hazardous and may cause dermal irritation. Pennyroyal is highly effective in repelling fleas but is toxic to the kidneys and nervous system. Additionally, avoid wormwood, it has been suggested for worm infestation, but it may cause renal failure, seizure and dermal toxicity.

Do not use oils on a dog who is seizure prone. Avoid their eyes, ears or too close to the nose, mucous membranes, or anal or genital areas. Now that we've spent so much time scaring you off it, we're going to move on to how to use the oils that are safe. Always double check before you purchase and apply the oils.

Topical application (on the skin) is the most commonly used technique and oils are applied directly to the areas needed. The oils penetrate the skin are quickly absorbed by tiny capillaries which carry them to the blood stream. The oils can be applied via massage or spritzers, spray and can be added to shampoos, conditioners, salves, ointments etc.

Petting is a less intense method of applying oils. Simply put the diluted oils on your hands, rub then together and stroke your dog. This is an excellent way of addressing emotional issues, such as anxiety, stress and depression. The oils work in conjunction with the touch. Do remember to ensure that your dog is happy with being stroked and that he indicates his permission to continue by you removing your hands and him signalling he wishes you to carry on. Watch his body language.

Diffusion and inhalation: diffusers are used to evaporate the oils which are inhaled. Try twenty to thirty minutes, maybe twice a day for a week. This is a great way to help Fido is he is not ready for touch. Always allow Fido to choose if he wants the treatment, allow him to move away from the scent. If you are diffusing, then allow him to leave the room. Use less on smaller dogs and puppies and do check with a holistic veterinarian before using on a pregnant dog.

Solving behavioural problems in dogs, no matter what they are, should be done with patience, care and love.

Sometimes they can be caused by physical problems, sudden aggression is an example. Dogs who are in pain may get aggressive especially when being touched. It could be owing to an injury, oral problems, ear infections, joint pain, arthritis etc. Some diseases that influence the brain may cause aggression. Example include autoimmune thyroiditis, encephalitis, hypoglycaemia, brain tumours or head injury.

Older dogs may have more aches and pain, their hearing is getting poorer and may be startled easily. Senior dogs may develop cognitive dysfunction. Males dogs around a female in season, may fight. A female may show maternal aggression towards anyone that approaches their puppies. Remember take in the context.

Poor nutrition may result in poor brain function. Under-socialised puppies and those who have had traumatic or fearful experiences during socialization period are more likely to develop fear and aggression related issues as adults.

Dogs that have been abused, punished excessively or neglected in the past may be fearful and aggressive. Reconsider those alpha roles. Overactive children with unpredictable behaviour to the dog, improper training and inconsistent leadership results in dogs that are confused about their relationship. They end up in a state of insecurity.

A holistic approach will consider a medical check-up and examining the diet. Perhaps switch to a natural high-quality food, maybe organic and home-made with natural supplements. Ensure that your dog gets the correct amount of exercise whilst allowing plenty of rest and sleep, training and playing games.

We need to treat dog behavioural problems holistically, to look at and deal with all the possibilities that may be at the root of the issue. Natural remedies such as herbs, homeopathic remedies, and essential oils can be used to help with emotions.

Herbs: Chamomile or lemon balm help to lift Fido's mood and make him happier and more secure. Holy Basil or Ashwagandha can help with stress.

Natural supplements: vitamin B6 can help with serotonin production. Gamma-aminobutyric Acid deficiency can result in anxiety and panic attacks. 5-hydroxytrytohan (5HTP) increases serotonin to help guard against fear, aggression and anxiety.

Essential oils: Consider a blend: 1 oz (30 ml) carrier oil, three drops lavender, two drops roman chamomile. One drop Sweet Marjoram. Place four or five drops of the blend on a bandanna around Fido's neck, once daily. You can also use the application methods given above. Remember Fido's permission.

Flower Essences: Thesehave been gaining popularity as a natural remedy to support and maintain the mental health of pets. In particular, with emotional issues that may leash to behavioural problems. Flower essences are extracts made from flowers and plants. They mainly work on an energetic level and have positive effects on mental and emotional levels. The essences use parts of different kinds of flowers, plants, trees and bushes to make extracts which are then diluted and potentized to become effective.

Bach first developed the flower essences, he identified thirty-eight healing plants. These are still available today, each for tackling a specific range of emotional and behavioural issue. Other essences have been developed by other companies. There are now special blends of flower essences specifically concocted to treat common dog problems.

The essences gently restore the balance between mind and body by getting rid of negative emotions such as fear or anxiety, which interfere with the equilibrium of the being as a whole. As the mind is balanced and relaxed, the body becomes stronger and has greater ability to self-heal. They help fine tune our dogs mentally and emotionally, allowing them to experience a higher standard of health and wellbeing.

Essences can be used to adjust different temperaments such as aggression, hyperactivity and anxiety. Thus, they can help against the struggle with excessive barking or chewing. They can be used in conjunction with other medications to aid treatment of physical ailments such as seizures, skin issuers and arthritis.

The best known one is Rescue Remedy which combines five original essences for synergistic effects and is used for emergencies and first aid situations for stress and trauma etc. Simply add four drops to drinking water during any time of stress. It is totally surprising how well it works, even allowing for seeing what we want to see.

Flower Essences have no side effects and can be used alongside other healing treatments to promote overall wellbeing.

Administering Essences: Simply drip the essence into the mouth or on the nose. Ensure the dropper does not touch the skin or mouth. Another option is to put in water. You can rub in onto skin in areas such as the inner ear flap or pads. Finally, you can use a spritzer and mix with distilled water and spray near the dog.

Flower essences generally work very quickly but as always it is unique to each individual. Be observant. Monitor his response and take any follow up actions. Do remember that often emotional imbalances such as depression or aggression can be due to an underlying physical problem. Before using an essence to treat the secondary symptom (the emotion) do check with your vet, this is not for acute or serious health problems in isolation.

Herbal treatment for dogs

Western medicine usually looks at a disease in isolation. A cure is to remove or suppress its symptom as quickly as possible. Perhaps with antibiotics, but these can greatly weaken Fido immune system, which leads to more health problems later. The holistic approach is the body, mind and life spirit when diagnosing the deeper underlying cause or causes of a disease.

Herbs are used for strengthening the weakened, or diseased, organ systems. They regulate and boost the immune system and return out of sync body functions to a state of normalcy which results in long lasting health.

Herbs contain chemicals which can have medicinal effects when used appropriately. When several herbs are used in combination, they have even more powerful effect on the long-term health. They boost the immune system, harmonize the body, detoxify, are nerve calming, relieve pain and add nutritious value to the diet.

As a general guide to amount, start slowly with low doses. Monitor the results and gradually increase according to reaction. Search for Dr Kids guide. It is a good idea to have five days on and two days off. Try for four weeks and then give a week off, unless you are treating a chronic health problem; in which case, continue without the week off. You can experiment with different herbs that you have discovered have similar effects.

Herbs are generally slow acting so expect sixty to ninety days to see a significant improvement. They are best used to support and improve general wellbeing, for chronic disease rather than emergency situations. Obtain the best quality herbs from reputable suppliers.

Acupuncture

This health treatment was developed about five thousand years ago by the Chinese. By inserting tiny metal needles into specific point called acupoints in the body physiological changes are made. They control and suppress pain while stimulating organs or body parts.

Acupoints are found along pathways called meridians, which connect the entire body and through which the 'Qi' or life force energy circulates. The meridians are deep in the body in many places. They surface at certain points on the skin, these acupoints are where the meridians can be easily accessed to create change.

There are twelve major meridians and three hundred and sixty-five acupoints in the body. In Eastern medicine the thinking is that disorders or diseases occurs when the 'Qi' is out of balance. Acupuncture is one way to stimulate the body to release its own pain relieving and anti-inflammatory substances to rebalance the body and create harmony.

Acupressure uses the same principles and knowledge, but without needles. Instead pressure is applied with the fingers. Red-light therapy can be used instead, or in addition, to pressure in order to further enhance the effect. This is very exciting since with study, you can learn the acupoints yourself and either use acupressure techniques or red-light therapy.

Acupressure (Shiatsu is a Japanese kind of acupressure), red light therapy using acupoints and acupuncture can help with Pain caused by arthritis, injuries, cancer etc.

Boosting the immune system; therapies using acupoints are very safe and have no side effects. There is a licence required and formal training for acupuncture. The efficacy will vary depending on experience and technique, the condition of the dog, how serious the problem, and the number, length and consistency of treatments.

It is relatively easy to learn where the bladder meridian line goes and the acupressure points, to massage the length is very beneficial towards wellbeing and well worth integrating into a weekly care schedule. Plus, of course, the massage component helps build the relationship.

Remember to obtain consent from Fido, otherwise it will be a stressful experience and detract from the healing effect and your relationship.

Homeopathy

This was developed originally by Samuel Hahnemann about two hundred years ago. Based on the principle of like cures like. This means that a substance that can cause certain symptoms in a healthy body can cure similar symptoms in an unhealthy one. Homeopathy aims to aid and stimulate Fido own defence and immune process. It uses small doses of specially prepared potentised, highly diluted remedies to set the body systems back to balance and stimulate the body's own energy towards healing. Remedies are derived from plants, animal materials and minerals. These remedies are prescribed to fit the needs of each individual, given in very small doses, used for prevention and treatment.

Homeopathic remedies do need to be selected properly and used in moderate potencies for a limited period. It's best under the guidance of a holistic vet. Homeopathy for dogs is best used to treat chronic ailments. Such remedies can be very effective in the treatment of acute ailments and injuries such as diarrhoea, bleeding, bites and stings. The action of a correctly selected homeopathic remedy can be faster than any other medicine.

Such remedies can be given to Fido by dropping the pellets into his mouth, dissolving them in a small amount of water or grinding them into a powder that is poured into the mouth.

Do not handle the pellets or mix into food. Administer the remedies at least an hour before food, avoid other medications especially allopathic medicine whilst Fido is having homeopathic treatment. If you wish to combine these with herbal remedies consult your homeopathic vet. Consult your homeopathic vet before allowing vaccinations whilst on homeopathic treatment.

Energy Therapies

Reiki. Crystal therapy, colour therapy

Reiki, Crystal and Colour therapy are also used for general wellbeing. The knowledge of meridians, acupoints and chakras are needed. We generally combine reiki with crystal therapy, combining reiki when massaging

The advantage of energy therapies is that they can be utilised without touch. This is very helpful when Fido finds touch aversive. Again, always ask permission. Although we are not touching physically, we are working in Fido's energy field and he will feel that. If he is uncomfortable, he will move away. We can always try again another time, when he may give permission.

Investigate what courses there may be in your area, we do recommend that you take a course that has some practical aspect. This will involve travel and more commitment, but it is totally worth it.

The Heart Connection

The heart connection(as explained by Kathy Kawalec of Dancing Hearts Dog Academy) exercises will help you to shift your perspective, to open the door to your mind and your heart so that you can see the world through the eyes of Fido. This shift is where a true heart to heart connection happens, where the seeds of partnership are planted for true collaborative partnership.

Tune in to what your heart is telling you. Spend fifteen to thirty minutes, choose a relaxing place, take several deep breaths, picture Fido's face, allow a smile as you feel the love and connection that you share. Think of a happy time that you and Fido enjoy together. Remember that time, allowing for the happiness to enter your heart. Put your hand on your heart to bring awareness and help you state your intentions to bypass your mind. Imagine a connection between your heart and Fido's heart.

Answer three questions:

- What are three things you love about Fido?
- What are three things you love about your partnership with Fido?
- Where are you and Fido having communication success in three areas?
- Think of a struggle that you and Fido are experiencing, can you identify where there is a communication breakdown?
- Where is the specific place where communication breaks down and what happens?
- Close your eyes and imagine what Fido might be experiencing when this happens: 3 things.
  - Where can you more closely listen your Fido's feed-back, list three things.
  - How can you modify and deepen the dialog loop in this situation, list three things.
  - What is your takeaway from this exercise? How has your perspective shifted? How will this shift deepen your heart connection with Fido?
  - What 3 things will you do right away to begin to shift the struggle

This heart connection exercise is simply one example of how we can connect with our dogs on a deeper level. There is so much more to discover. Sonia's work as a healer using energy therapies has helped to give a glimpse of how we can help our dog in so many ways, on so many levels.

Make a vow: I will not experience over-whelm. I will experience excitement.

A Brief Case Study

Sally contacted Sonia for help with her family of rescue dogs. Sally devotes her life to her dogs, whilst she reported that her dogs do bark 'quite a bit' she has no neighbours and does not mind if it becomes a little noisy. She was worried because two of her girls, Molly and Jill, had a couple of fights. No need for veterinary attention but enough to be concerned.

General group stress bucket level was discussed, along with gated communities to keep Molly and Jill separated. It was believed that resource guarding was the trigger. Susan was shown games to help with resource guarding (general optimism plus plenty of toy switch games, taking care to always end with scatter feeding in order to have a reward at the end of any game). Managing the environment regarding availability of toys and supervision was discussed. Only having access to the toys with supervision, monitoring body language and excitement level was implemented.

Susan decided to have regular quiet periods throughout the day, she encouraged her dogs to rest by closing curtains, playing soothing music and using aromatherapy and some herbal preparations. She was shown how to give a calming massage to her dogs always checking for consent and allowing each dog to choose the oil used. She noticed that certain dogs seemed to prefer specific scents on a regular basis. Susan then investigated Bach flower remedies. She learned some simple acupressure techniques that she incorporated into the massage.

Susan has changed the diet away from prepared kibble and feeds a more natural diet. She keeps individual information sheets listing the quantity and type of food including any herbs.

Susan reports that the issue between the two girls Jill and Molly has been resolved though she continues to ensure she supervises carefully. She continues to have several quiet periods throughout the day so each dog can sleep and empty their individual stress bucket.

Her household is much more harmonious now and, although she was not concerned about the barking, she notes it is much more peaceful. Susan says she particularly enjoys giving each dog someone-to-one time with their massage. She believes this has been very important allowing her to focus on each dog and assessing their physical and emotional state.

Summary

In this chapter we have briefly introduced:

- Some Holistic Therapies, essential oils, herbal treatment and the heart connection as some examples of how we can connect with our dog.
- There are so many ways we can learn help our dogs be safe, calm and happy. We hope you will be excited to learn more.
- Remember: I vow to not experience over-whelm. I vow to experience excitement.

Mythbuster Moment: Alternative therapies are not likely to be helpful when training our dog.

Working on all levels holistic therapies are a very powerful aid to help with your dog training.

THANK YOU FOR READING!

As you have seen, this book is divided into four sections: The Dog End of the leash, Managing the Environment, Perfect Partnership and last but definitely, not least The Human End of the Leash.

Whilst we have divided our approach into four sections that is only to help you to organise and process the information. Clearly all four elements interact, boundaries are artificial, we work on all four components at the same time.

Keep yourself, the environment and your dog safe, calm and happy. Have fun playing the games. You will have the best partnership and your dog will make the best choices - the ones you want him to make. Say good-bye to the struggles and turn them into strengths.

For extra, bespoke, one-to-one support, we would love to meet you on our on-line course and closed Facebook group. We will guide you with live coaching calls and interactive, motivational resources to help keep you on track and having fun. For you and your dog to be the best versions of yourselves. We wish you well with your journey.

If you'd like to see your methods in action, please go to www.deviant-2dream.dog for three free videos. Additionally, you can join our Facebook community 'Deviant2Dream.Dog Family' from there. If you feel you need a more bespoke tuition for training your own Fido, please have a look at our online course which will dig deeper and provide extra support and coaching.

GLOSSARY OF TERMS

95% rule – Do not ask your dog to do anything you are not 95% certain he will do. Would you bet £500, for example, that he will recall off the rabbit? Are you 95% sure he will recall of the rabbit? If you are not 95% sure or that you would not bet £500 he will recall then do NOT give the recall cue.

Baby steps – Within your interactions with your dog, ensure that when you are increasing the difficulty of the task you only do so in tiny amounts. Only change one thing at a time. The size of the steps will vary depending on the dog. Train the dog in front of you and make adjustments as you need. If you and your dog have not been successful, then take that as information and make the steps smaller.

Bikejoring – A sport or leisure activity where your dog pulls a bicycle. Specialist harness and lines are used. Training will be required as this can be a high-risk activity. This is perfect for high energy dogs that cannot be allowed off lead.

Boundary/bed/mat – This refers to any area you or your dog chooses to settle. A boundary can be anything. Usually it is a mat, towel, dog bed, raised bed or crate. You and your dog can generalise the concept to mean anything either of you chooses. On a walk this may be a tree stump, low wall, boulder. At home you could choose to have the dog bed as a boundary where he chooses to relax. You can also cue for the boundary and expect your dog to remain there until he is released. See boundary and crate training.

Calming signals – These are signals whereby dogs communicate with each other. They try to use them with us too but sadly we often miss them, or don't realise they are trying to communicate. Essentially your dog is saying, 'hey I am no threat to you, calm down'. We mention these in chapter 1.4.

Calmness Circle – This includes the 'Calming Activities', 'Calmness Procedure and Games' and 'Crate or Boundary Rest' from chapter 1.3.

Circles of emotions – In a 24-hour day a dog should have 18 hours rest. We want to work towards your dog sleeping and resting for at least 16 hours a day. A puppy will need more. The circle of emotion can be sectioned into high energy activities which may lead to your dog going over threshold. Whilst some high energy activities can be seen as positive, we need to ensure that the dog is in 'Happy Land' first – experiencing positive emotions. Most dogs do not have enough sleep and relaxing activities, they have too much time spent being over stimulated and vigilant, thereby going over threshold. This is explained more in chapter 1.3.

Clicker – A small piece of equipment that when pressed gives a clear click. This is to mark when your dog makes a desired movement.

Clicker training – In order the click to be viewed as positive reinforcement and be effective previous training must be given. The clicker needs to be sounded just before your dog is given positive reinforcement. Such pairing will be over many trials until Fido is rewarded by the click alone. It will still be necessary to do some positive reward to keep the positive association with the click.

Crate – Any enclosure designed for animals with the intention of being a safe, secure place. Crates will have a door that can be secured to prevent your dog from leaving the space. You can choose to leave the door open for free access (using it as a boundary/bed) or close it to ensure his safety and rest.

Five F's – Flight, Fight, Freeze, Flirt and Flock. These refer to the dog's emotions such as Fear or Rage and the subsequent behaviour that animals exhibit. For dogs, depending on breed, previous learning and personality, they will have preferred responses.

- Fight to directly confront or respond to confrontation by fighting.
- Flight is to respond by quickly giving distance.
- Freeze can be a momentary stillness before choosing one of the other responses or remaining still.
- Flirt is a less popularly well-known response where a dog chooses some other behaviour, often it will seem to be playful. If coming from a place of fear it can quickly change to one of the other F's for example Fight.
- Flock refers to the propensity to seek companionship and proximity usually with the same species. With our canine companion it is likely to be he runs to you for comforting.

Flexibility– Playing the games to enhance your dog's flexibility will help him to give a more desired response in place of the original undesired response. As he develops this ability, he will be able to think through options instead of simply doing what he has always done.

Frustration– The ability to deal with frustration. A large amount of undesirable behaviour is exhibited by a dog in response to him feeling frustrated. If we can develop his ability to deal with frustration and not feel the negative emotion (grow a larger bucket) he will remain calm and his behaviour will come out of the calmness box. This will be desirable behaviour.

Gated communities – A useful way of ensuring a harmonious and peaceful multi-dog household. Using crates, boundaries, doors and baby gates to separate the dogs into different areas, rooms etc. One key example of managing the environment.

Judgment bias test – This is a test to establish if an animal is expecting a negative outcome or positive outcome (see pessimism and optimism). Pessimism has survival value in the wild, but in our human world the optimistic dog is better adapted.

Multi-dog household – More than one dog living in the household (or more than one dog being present in the household such as visiting dogs).

Ninja feeding – This refers to stealth feeding lower value reward, to reinforce the calmness whilst avoiding suggesting it is time to interact with you. This takes practice.

Pessimism and optimism – We are used to thinking about these characteristics as appertaining to humans. They can readily be applied to animals. As with humans, dogs can be either inherently pessimistic (expecting a negative outcome) or optimistic (expecting a positive outcome). Pessimism can exhibit as undesirable behaviour. We can help move Fido toward optimism by playing the games.

Rehearse the room – If you want a room to be a place where your dog settles and does not anticipate play time, then be consistent. Boundary and crate games in the room where you want your dog to be calm. Games with higher excitement and interest can be played in other rooms, the garden or on the walks. It is generally a good idea to rehearse the car as being a place to settle and sleep. This is introduced in 2.1.

Relationship Bank Account – Think of your bank account, when you pay into it (make a deposit) you have done something positive, when you make a withdrawal you deplete the account. When you play a fun game, you have done a positive relationship enhancing activity, when you punish or intimidate your dog you have done a negative relationship depleting activity. A withdrawal inevitably occurs but it is not final, you can ensure you have many positive interactions to keep the relationship bank account with your dog in credit.

Ritualised signals – Calming signals are one example of ritualised signals. Ritualised signals are used throughout the animal kingdom for communication. They have been studied extensively especially with courtship behaviour and how animals use them to avoid conflict.

Rules of engagement – Think in terms of teamwork and partnership, not hierarchy and dominance. This was also discussed in 2.1, this is a term we use to manage the interactions with your dogs. Especially when introducing a new dog to a multi-dog household.

Sad Land and Happy Land – This refers to the concept that the world can be divided into a place where positive, happy, bright emotions are felt and/or negative, sad, dark emotions. Many dogs may spend much of their time in a low intensity sad, dark side. Our aim is to shape their brains through games to the other happy, bright side.

Scatter feeding – Choosing to feed some of your dog's daily allowance of food by scattering the chosen amount onto the floor, garden, grass or even into and over toys. This is a calming activity which engages the nose and brain. You can select any value of food to scatter to suit your purpose and individual dog.

Shaping – A training technique where incremental movements made by your dog towards the desired goal are rewarded. Explained in chapter 3.2.

Shaping – Breaking a piece of behaviour down into tiny increments and rewarding each movement towards your goal. Often clickers are utilised with behaviour shaping. Alternatively, a 'yes' or a 'nice' marking can be used.

Sleep – Refer back to the circle of emotions in the glossary. A dog should have at least 16 hours a day sleeping and resting.

Stress bucket – An analogy to help us to picture how incremental amounts of stress, no matter how small or even if seen as positive, contribute to the cortisol (stress hormone) level raising. This can result in your dog becoming 'over threshold'. Being over threshold is highly likely to result in him choosing less-desirable behaviour, and being unable to think, learn or listen to you. For a more detailed explanation see chapter 1.3.

Use the 95% rule in all your interactions with your dog, never ask more than he can give at that moment.

Valence – We mainly talk about this in chapter 1.3, Valence is the type of emotion felt, positive or negative which is pared with the level of arousal or excitement.

Yerkes/Dodson Law (curve) – To ensure we can keep Fido in his thinking zone, we have to ensure that we are aware of how much excitement (arousal) is the right amount. Too much and he is over the top of the curve and his performance will diminish. Too little and he will also not be at the top of his game. For more information see chapter 1.3.

Zoomies – This has become a widely used, popular term to refer to a dog running at high speed, often in circles, spinning, jumping and generally using a great deal of energy. It can be amusing to watch but it can also lead to accidents. On the whole, it's best to avoid zoomies and interrupt the behaviour. It can be a sign that the dog is over-stimulated and could make some undesirable choices.

Lightning Source UK Ltd.
Milton Keynes UK
UKHW010630061020
371100UK00001B/129